2 OOPS! DROPPED HER HALO ANGEL
5 REINDEER ORNAMENT
7 MINI CLOTHESPIN ANGEL
8 DANGLE SANTA
11 STOCKING
12 SANTA ORNAMENT
15 DOLL PINS
20 DOOR KNOB WREATH
21 SANTA ORNAMENT & PIN
26 SNOWMAN ORNAMENT & PIN
28 HOLLY LAPEL PIN
29 GENERAL INSTRUCTIONS
32 THREAD INFORMATION


Miniature marvels in colorful thread crochet make fun holiday decorations. Hang them on the tree, present them as little gifts or package adornments, display them in a table arrangement, or wear one as a lapel pin. Ribbons and other trims add charm.

LEISURE ARTS, INC. • Maumelle, Arkansas

# OOPS! DROPPED HER HALO ANGEL

EASY +

**Finished Height:** Approximately 3¾" (9.5 cm)

## SHOPPING LIST

### Thread (Lace Weight)

LACE 0

- ☐ White - 50 yards (45.5 meters)
- ☐ Metallic Gold - 18 yards (16.5 meters)
- ☐ Cream - 7 yards (6.5 meters)

### Crochet Hook

- ☐ Steel, size 8 (1.5 mm)

### Additional Supplies

- ☐ Tapestry needle
- ☐ Polyester fiberfill
- ☐ Craft glue
- ☐ ¾" (19 mm) gold ring
- ☐ 1/8" (3 mm) wide gold ribbon - 12" (30.5 cm) length
- ☐ Black seed beads (for eyes) - 2
- ☐ Sewing needle & thread
- ☐ Small gold ribbon roses - 2
- ☐ Tiny jingle bells - 4
- ☐ Size G (4 mm) crochet hook (for Bangs)

***Gauge is not important for this design.***

## STITCH GUIDE

**DOUBLE CROCHET 2 TOGETHER** ***(abbreviated dc2tog)*** (uses next 2 dc)

★ YO, insert hook in **next** dc, YO and pull up a loop, YO and draw through 2 loops on hook; repeat from ★ once **more**, YO and draw through all 3 loops on hook **(counts as one dc)**.

## HEAD

**Rnd 1** (Right side)**:** With Cream, ch 4, 9 dc in fourth ch from hook **(3 skipped chs count as first dc)**; join with slip st to first dc: 10 dc.

*Note:* Loop a short piece of thread around any stitch to mark Rnd 1 as **right** side.

**Rnd 2:** Ch 3 **(counts as first dc, now and throughout unless otherwise specified)**, dc in same st as joining, 2 dc in next dc and in each dc around; join with slip st to first dc: 20 dc.

**Rnd 3:** Ch 3, dc in next dc and in each dc around; join with slip st to first dc.

**Rnd 4:** Ch 2, dc in next dc, dc2tog around; skip beginning ch-2 and join with slip st to first dc: 10 dc.

Stuff Head with polyester fiberfill.

**Rnd 5:** Ch 2, dc in next dc, dc2tog around; skip beginning ch-2 and join with slip st to first dc, finish off: 5 dc.

## DRESS

**Rnd 1:** With **right** side facing, join White with dc in same st as joining *(see Joining With Dc, page 30)*; dc in same st, 2 dc in next dc and in each dc around; join with slip st to first dc: 10 dc.

**Rnd 2:** Ch 3, dc in same st as joining, 2 dc in next dc and in each dc around; join with slip st to first dc: 20 dc.

**Rnd 3:** Ch 3, dc in next 3 dc, 2 dc in next dc, (dc in next 4 dc, 2 dc in next dc) around; join with slip st to first dc: 24 dc.

**Rnds 4 and 5:** Ch 3, dc in next dc and in each dc around; join with slip st to first dc.

**Rnd 6:** Ch 3, dc in same st as joining and in next 3 dc, (2 dc in next dc, dc in next 3 dc) around; join with slip st to first dc: 30 dc.

**Rnd 7:** Ch 3, dc in same st as joining and in next 4 dc, (2 dc in next dc, dc in next 4 dc) around; join with slip st to first dc: 36 dc.

**Rnd 8:** Ch 3, dc in same st as joining and in next 5 dc, (2 dc in next dc, dc in next 5 dc) around; join with slip st to first dc: 42 dc.

**Rnd 9:** Ch 3, working in BLO ***(Fig. 2, page 30)***, dc in same st as joining and in next 6 dc, (2 dc in next dc, dc in next 6 dc) around; join with slip st to **both** loops of first dc, do **not** finish off: 48 dc.

**TRIM**

**Rnd 1:** Ch 1, working in FLO ***(Fig. 2, page 30)***, sc in same st as joining, ch 3, (sc in next dc, ch 3) around; join with slip st to **both** loops of first sc, finish off.

**Rnd 2:** With **right** side facing, Head toward you, and working in free loops on Rnd 8 of Dress ***(Fig. 3a, page 30)***, join White with sc in any st ***(see Joining With Sc, page 30)***; ch 3, (sc in next st, ch 3) around; join with slip st to **both** loops of first sc, finish off.

## ARM (Make 2)

**Rnd 1:** With White, ch 4, 5 dc in fourth ch from hook **(3 skipped chs count as first dc)**; join with slip st to first dc: 6 dc.

*Note:* Mark Rnd 1 as **right** side.

**Rnd 2:** Ch 3, dc in same st as joining, 2 dc in next dc and in each dc around; join with slip st to first dc: 12 dc.

**Rnds 3-5:** Ch 3, dc in next dc and in each dc around; join with slip st to first dc.

**Trim:** Ch 1, working in FLO, sc in same st as joining, ch 3, (sc in next dc, ch 3) around; join with slip st to **both** loops of first sc, finish off.

**Hand:** With **right** side facing, Rnd 1 of Arm toward you and working in free loops on Rnd 5 of Arm, join Cream with dc in any st; dc in next st and in each st around; join with slip st to first dc, finish off leaving a 6" (15 cm) end for sewing.

Thread tapestry needle with end and weave through sts on Hand ***(Fig. 6, page 31)***. Pull tightly to close and secure end.

**Arm Tie:** With White and leaving a 4" (10 cm) end, ch 10; finish off leaving a 4" (10 cm) end. Thread ch through Rnd 1 of Arm and around any dc on Rnd 2 of Dress; tie ends together on **wrong** side.

For second Arm, skip 9 dc on Rnd 2 of Dress and tie second Arm around next dc in same manner.

**Hanger:** With White and leaving a 4" (10 cm) end, ch 35; finish off leaving a 4" (10 cm) end. Thread through Hand of left Arm; tie ends in a knot. Hide ends through Hand and Arm.

## LEG (Make 2)

**Rnd 1:** With White, ch 4, 7 dc in fourth ch from hook **(3 skipped chs count as first dc)**; join with slip st to first dc: 8 dc.

*Note:* Mark Rnd 1 as **right** side.

**Rnds 2-7:** Ch 3, dc in next dc and in each dc around; join with slip st to first dc.

**Trim:** Ch 1, working in FLO, sc in same st as joining, ch 3, (sc in next dc, ch 3) around; join with slip st to **both** loops of first sc.

**Foot:** Ch 1, working in free loops on Rnd 7 of Leg, slip st in first st (behind Trim), ch 3, dc in next dc and in each dc around; join with slip st to first dc, finish off leaving a 6" (15 cm) end for sewing.

Thread tapestry needle with end and weave through sts on Foot. Pull tightly to close and secure end.

**Leg Tie:** With White and leaving a 4" (10 cm) end, ch 20; finish off leaving a 4" (10 cm) end. Thread ch through Rnd 1 of Leg and around dc on Rnd 2 of inside of Dress; tie ends together on **wrong** side.

## WINGS

### FIRST WING

With White, ch 5; join with slip st to form a ring.

**Row 1:** Ch 3, 5 dc in ring; do **not** join: 6 dc.

**Row 2** (Right side)**:** Ch 3, turn; dc in first dc, 2 dc in next dc and in each dc across: 12 dc.

*Note:* Mark Row 2 as **right** side.

**Row 3:** Ch 3, turn; dc in first dc, 2 dc in next dc and in each dc across: 24 dc.

**Row 4** (Beading row)**:** Ch 3 **(counts as first hdc plus ch 1)**, hdc in next dc, ★ ch 1, skip next dc, hdc in next dc; repeat from ★ across: 12 ch-1 sps.

**Row 5:** Ch 1, turn; sc in first hdc, 2 sc in each ch-1 sp across: 25 sc.

**Row 6:** Ch 1, turn; sc in first sc, ★ skip next 2 sc, 5 dc in next sc, skip next 2 sc, sc in next sc; repeat from ★ across; finish off.

### SECOND WING

**Row 1:** With **wrong** side facing, join White with dc in ring; 5 dc in ring; do **not** join: 6 dc.

Complete same as first Wing.

Wings may be stiffened if desired. Weave ribbon through beading row; sew or glue ends to secure.

## HAT

### TOP

**Rnd 1** (Right side)**:** With White, ch 2, 6 sc in second ch from hook; do **not** join, place marker to indicate beginning of rnd ***(see Markers, page 30)***.

*Note:* Mark Rnd 1 as **right** side.

**Rnd 2:** 2 Sc in each sc around: 12 sc.

**Rnd 3:** (2 Sc in next sc, sc in next sc) around: 18 sc.

**Rnd 4:** (2 Sc in next sc, sc in next 2 sc) around: 24 sc.

### SIDES

**Rnd 1:** Slip st in BLO of next sc, ch 3, dc in BLO of each sc around; join with slip st to **both** loops of first dc.

**Rnd 2:** Ch 3, dc in next 3 dc, dc2tog, (dc in next 4 dc, dc2tog) around; join with slip st to first dc: 20 dc.

### BRIM

**Rnd 1:** Ch 3, dc in same st as joining, 2 dc in next dc and in each dc around; join with slip st to first dc: 40 dc.

**Edging Rnd:** Ch 1, working from **left** to **right**, ★ insert hook in st to right of hook ***(Fig. A)***, YO and draw through, under and to left of loop on hook (2 loops on hook) ***(Fig. B)***, YO and draw through both loops on hook ***(Fig. C)*** **(reverse sc made, *Fig. D*)**; repeat from ★ around; join with slip st to first st, finish off.

**Fig. A**

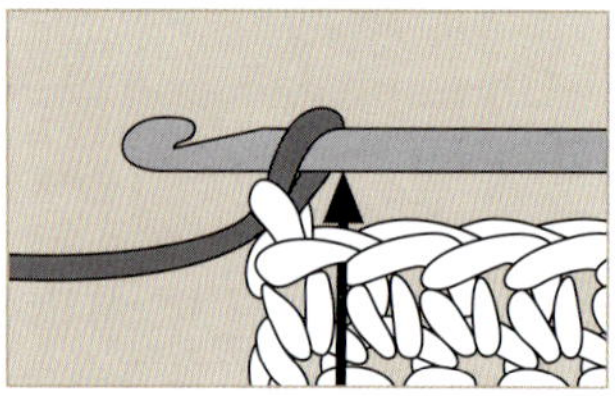

**Fig. B**

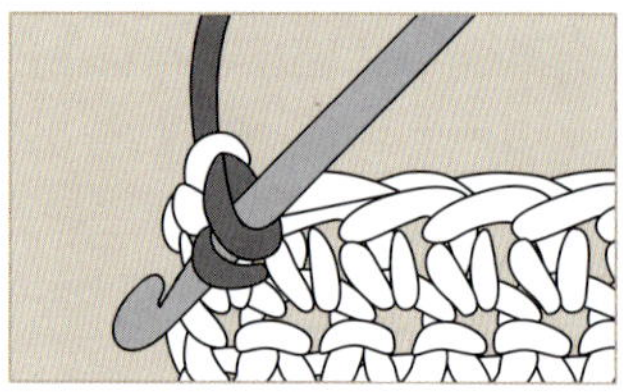

**Fig. C**

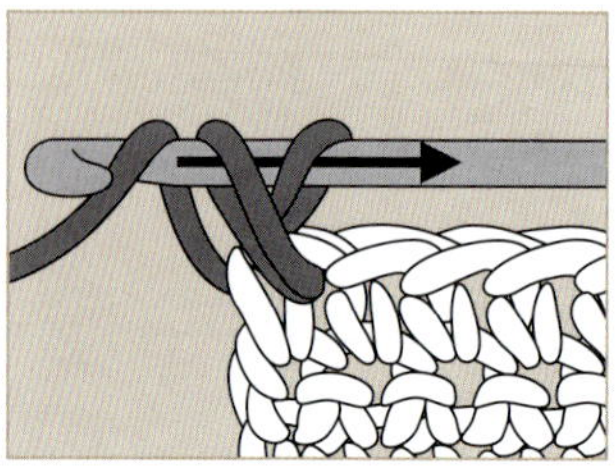

**Fig. D**

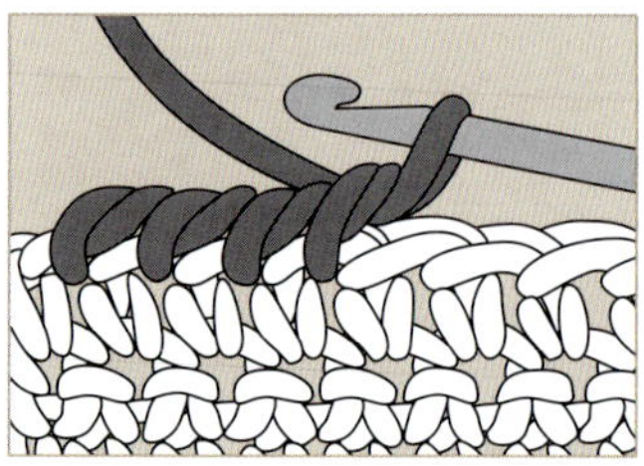

### HAIR

**PIGTAILS**

Cut a piece of cardboard 3" high x 5" wide (7.5 cm x 12.5 cm). Wind Metallic Gold approximately 60 times around the height of cardboard. Apply a line of craft glue across the thread at the top edge of the cardboard. When dry, cut loops at the bottom edge and remove from cardboard. Glue the dry line of glue across the center of the Head from front to back. Tie in pigtails and trim to desired length. Add small jingle bell to each tie.

**BANGS**

Wrap Metallic Gold approximate 20 times around the larger end of a size G crochet hook. Apply a line of glue across threads. When dry, slide Bangs from hook.
Glue dry line of glue across forehead.

Glue or sew pieces in place, using photo as a guide for placement, page 2:

- Add ribbon around neck.
- Attach Wings to back of Dress.
- Attach Hat to Head; then attach rose to Hat.
- Sew seed bead eyes to Head.
- Add ring (halo) to right Hand.
- Add remaining rose to dress and remaining jingle bells to Feet.

*Design by Patricia Pogue.*

# REINDEER ORNAMENT

EASY

**Finished Height:**
Approximately 3½" (9 cm)

## SHOPPING LIST

### Thread (Lace Weight) LACE 0

- ☐ Brown - 65 yards (59.5 meters)
- ☐ Black - small amount
- ☐ Off White - small amount
- ☐ Red - small amount

### Crochet Hook

- ☐ Steel, size 9 (1.4 mm)

### Additional Supplies

- ☐ Tapestry needle
- ☐ Polyester fiberfill
- ☐ Ribbon or twisted cord
- ☐ Metallic thread

***Gauge is not important for this design.***

### STITCH GUIDE

**SINGLE CROCHET 2 TOGETHER**
***(abbreviated sc2tog)***
Pull up a loop in each of next 2 sc, YO and draw through all 3 loops on hook **(counts as one sc)**.

### BODY

**Rnd 1** (Right side)**:** With Brown, ch 2, 8 sc in second ch from hook; do **not** join, place a marker to indicate beginning of rnd *(see Markers, page 30)*.

*Note:* Loop a short piece of thread around any stitch to mark Rnd 1 as **right** side.

**Rnd 2:** 2 Sc in each sc around: 16 sc.

**Rnd 3:** (Sc in next sc, 2 sc in next sc) around: 24 sc.

**Rnd 4:** Sc in each sc around.

**Rnd 5:** (Sc in next 2 sc, 2 sc in next sc) around: 32 sc.

**Rnd 6:** Sc in each sc around.

**Rnd 7:** (Sc in next 3 sc, 2 sc in next sc) around: 40 sc.

**Rnds 8-27:** Sc in each sc around.

**Rnd 28:** (Sc in next 3 sc, sc2tog) around: 32 sc.

**Rnd 29:** Sc in each sc around.

**Rnd 30:** (Sc in next 2 sc, sc2tog) around: 24 sc.

**Rnd 31:** (Sc in next sc, sc2tog) around: 16 sc.

Stuff Body with polyester fiberfill.

**Rnd 32:** Sc2tog around; slip st in next sc, finish off leaving an 8" (20.5 cm) length for sewing.

Thread needle with end and weave through sts on Rnd 32 ***(Fig. 6, page 31)***; pull tightly to close and secure end.

## HEAD

**Rnd 1** (Right side)**:** With Red, ch 2, 8 sc in second ch from hook; join with slip st to first sc changing to Off White ***(Fig. 4b, page 31)***, cut Red.

***Note:*** Mark Rnd 1 as **right** side.

**Rnd 2:** Ch 1, sc in same st as joining, 2 sc in next sc, (sc in next sc, 2 sc in next sc) around; join with slip st to first sc: 12 sc.

**Rnd 3:** Ch 1, sc in same st as joining and in each sc around; join with slip st to first sc changing to Brown, cut Off White.

**Rnd 4:** Ch 1, sc in same st as joining and in next sc, 2 sc in next sc, (sc in next 2 sc, 2 sc in next sc) around; do **not** join, place a marker to indicate beginning of rnd: 16 sc.

**Rnd 5:** (Sc in next 3 sc, 2 sc in next sc) around: 20 sc.

**Rnd 6:** (Sc in next 4 sc, 2 sc in next sc) around: 24 sc.

**Rnd 7:** Sc in each sc around.

**Rnd 8:** (Sc in next 5 sc, 2 sc in next sc) around: 28 sc.

**Rnd 9:** Sc in each sc around.

**Rnd 10:** (Sc in next 6 sc, 2 sc in next sc) around: 32 sc.

**Rnds 11-18:** Sc in each sc around.

**Rnd 19:** (Sc in next 2 sc, sc2tog) around: 24 sc.

**Rnd 20:** (Sc in next sc, sc2tog) around: 16 sc.

Stuff Head with polyester fiberfill.

**Rnd 21:** Sc2tog around; slip st in next sc, finish off leaving an 8" (20.5 cm) length for sewing.

Thread needle with end and weave through sts on Rnd 21. Pull tightly to close and secure end.

## LEG (Make 4)

**Rnd 1** (Right side)**:** With Black, ch 2, 8 sc in second ch from hook; join with slip st to first sc.

***Note:*** Mark Rnd 1 as **right** side.

**Rnd 2:** Ch 1, sc in same st as joining, 2 sc in next sc, (sc in next sc, 2 sc in next sc) around; join with slip st to first sc changing to Brown, cut Black: 12 sc.

**Rnd 3:** Ch 1, sc in same st as joining and in each sc around; do **not** join, place a marker to indicate beginning of rnd.

**Rnds 4-16:** Sc in each sc around; at end of Rnd 16, slip st in next sc, finish off leaving a 10" (25.5 cm) length for sewing.

## EAR (Make 2)

With Brown, ch 6.

**Row 1:** Sc in second ch from hook and in each ch across: 5 sc.

**Row 2** (Right side)**:** Ch 1, turn; beginning in first sc, sc2tog, sc in last 3 sc: 4 sc.

***Note:*** Mark Row 2 as **right** side.

**Row 3:** Ch 1, turn; beginning in first sc, sc2tog, sc in last 2 sc: 3 sc.

**Row 4:** Ch 1, turn; pull up a loop in each of 3 sc, YO and draw through all 4 loops on hook: one st.

**Edging Rnd:** Ch 1, do **not** turn; sc evenly around entire piece; join with slip st to first sc, finish off.

## TAIL

Work same as Ear.

Using photo as a guide for placement, page 5:

- Sew Head to Body.
- With Brown, sew Ears to Head 3 sc apart, and Tail to Body.
- Stuff Legs with polyester fiberfill and sew to Body.
- Embroider eyes on Head.

## ANTLERS

With Black, ch 7, slip st in back ridge of second ch from hook and each ch across ***(Fig. 1, page 30)***; sc around each sc between Ears; ch 7, slip st in back ridge of second ch from hook and each ch across, slip st in side of last sc worked; finish off.

Add ribbon or twisted cord around neck and tie in a bow.
Add metallic thread hanger.

*Design by Joan Beebe.*

# MINI CLOTHESPIN ANGEL

EASY

**Finished Height:** Approximately 2½" (6.5 cm) tall

## SHOPPING LIST

### Thread (Lace Weight)

LACE 0

- ☐ White - 15 yards (13.5 meters)
- ☐ Red - 10 yards (9 meters)
- ☐ Green - 5 yards (4.5 meters)

### Crochet Hook

- ☐ Steel, size 6 (1.8 mm)

### Additional Supplies

- ☐ Mini wooden clothespin
- ☐ Craft glue
- ☐ Tapestry needle
- ☐ Metallic thread

## GAUGE INFORMATION

20 sc = 2" (5 cm)

## BODICE

With White, leaving an 8" (20.5 cm) length and beginning at neck edge, ch 12; being careful **not** to twist ch, join with slip st to form a ring.

**Rnd 1** (Right side)**:** Ch 3 **(counts as first dc)**, dc in same ch as joining, 3 dc in next ch, (2 dc in next ch, 3 dc in next ch) around; join with slip st to first dc: 30 dc.

*Note:* Loop a short piece of thread around any stitch to mark Rnd 1 as **right** side.

**Rnd 2:** Ch 1, sc in same st as joining and in next 2 dc, ch 1, skip next 10 dc (wing), sc in next 5 dc, ch 1, skip next 10 dc (wing), sc in last 2 dc; join with slip st to first sc, do **not** finish off: 10 sc and 2 chs.

## SKIRT

**Rnd 1:** Ch 4 **(counts as first dc plus ch 1, now and throughout)**, dc in same st as joining, (dc, ch 1, dc) in next sc and in each sc and each ch around; join with slip st to first dc: 24 dc and 12 ch-1 sps.

**Rnd 2:** (Slip st, ch 4, dc) in next ch-1 sp, skip next dc, dc in sp **before** next dc ***(Fig. 5, page 31)***, ★ (dc, ch 1, dc) in next ch-1 sp, skip next dc, dc in sp **before** next dc; repeat from ★ around; join with slip st to first dc: 36 dc and 12 ch-1 sps.

**Rnd 3:** (Slip st, ch 4, dc) in next ch-1 sp, skip next dc, (dc, ch 1, dc) in next dc, ★ (dc, ch 1, dc) in next ch-1 sp, skip next dc, (dc, ch 1, dc) in next dc; repeat from ★ around; join with slip st to first dc, finish off: 48 dc and 12 ch-1 sps.

**Rnd 4:** With **right** side facing, join Red with dc in any ch-1 sp ***(see Joining With Dc, page 30)***; (ch 1, dc in same sp) twice, ★ dc in next ch-1 sp, (ch 1, dc in same sp) twice; repeat from ★ around; join with slip st to first dc, finish off.

**Trim:** With **right** side facing and neck edge toward you, join Green with sc around post of any dc on Rnd 3 ***(see Joining With Sc, page 30)***; ch 3, (sc around post of next dc on Rnd 3, ch 3) around; join with slip st to first sc, finish off.

## WING

**Rnd 1:** With **right** side facing and Skirt toward you, join White with dc in free loop of ch at underarm ***(Fig. 3b, page 30)***; ch 1, dc in same ch, (dc, ch 1, dc) in each skipped dc on Rnd 1 of Bodice; join with slip st to first dc, finish off: 22 dc and 11 ch-1 sps.

**Rnd 2:** With **right** side facing, join Red with dc in first ch-1 sp; ch 1, dc in same sp, skip next dc, dc in sp **before** next dc, ★ (dc, ch 1, dc) in next ch-1 sp, skip next dc, dc in sp **before** next dc; repeat from ★ around; join with slip st to first dc, finish off.

Repeat for second Wing.

**Neck Edging:** With **right** side facing, and working in free loops of beginning ch, insert hook in ch at base of long end, YO and pull up a loop with long end; slip st in next ch and in each ch around; join with slip st to first st, finish off.

## HALO

**Rnd 1** (Right side)**:** With White, ch 2, 12 sc in second ch from hook; join with slip st to first sc, finish off.

***Note:*** Mark Rnd 1 as **right** side.

**Rnd 2:** With **right** side facing, join Green with sc in same st as joining; ch 3, (sc in next sc, ch 3) around; join with slip st to first sc, finish off.

Place Dress onto clothespin; glue in place. Glue Halo to back of "head". Add metallic thread hanger.

*Design by Nanette M. Seale.*

# DANGLE SANTA

EASY +

**Finished Height:** Approximately 6¾"(17 cm)

## SHOPPING LIST

### Thread (Lace Weight) LACE 0

- ☐ Red - 50 yards (45.5 meters)
- ☐ White - 38 yards (34.5 meters)
- ☐ Cream - 5 yards (4.5 meters)
- ☐ Black - small amount

### Crochet Hook

- ☐ Steel, size 8 (1.5 mm)

### Additional Supplies

- ☐ Tapestry needle
- ☐ Polyester fiberfill
- ☐ Craft glue
- ☐ Black seed beads (for eyes) - 2
- ☐ Sewing needle & thread
- ☐ Silver glitter fabric paint (for Buckle)

***Gauge is not important for this design.***

## STITCH GUIDE

**BEGINNING POPCORN** (uses one st or sp)
Ch 3 **(counts as first dc)**, 4 dc in st or sp indicated, drop loop from hook, insert hook from **front** to **back** in first dc of 5-dc group, hook dropped loop and draw through st, ch 1 to close.

**POPCORN** (uses one st or sp)
5 Dc in st or sp indicated, drop loop from hook, insert hook from **front** to **back** in first dc of 5-dc group, hook dropped loop and draw through st, ch 1 to close.

## BODY

**Rnd 1** (Right side)**:** With Red, ch 4, 9 dc in fourth ch from hook **(3 skipped chs count as first dc)**; join with slip st to first dc: 10 dc.

***Note:*** Loop a short piece of thread around any stitch to mark Rnd 1 as **right** side.

**Rnd 2:** Ch 3 **(counts as first dc, now and throughout)**, dc in same st as joining, 2 dc in next dc and in each dc around; join with slip st to first dc: 20 dc.

**Rnd 3:** Ch 3, dc in same st as joining and in next dc, (2 dc in next dc, dc in next dc) around; join with slip st to first dc: 30 dc.

**Rnd 4:** Ch 3, dc in same st as joining and in next 2 dc, (2 dc in next dc, dc in next 2 dc) around; join with slip st to first dc changing to White ***(Fig. 4b, page 31)***, drop Red: 40 dc.

**Rnd 5:** With White, work Beginning Popcorn in same st as joining, skip next dc, (work Popcorn in next dc, skip next dc) around; join with slip st to top of Beginning Popcorn changing to Red, cut White: 20 Popcorns.

**Rnd 6:** Ch 3, dc in next ch-1 closing and in each Popcorn and ch-1 closing around; join with slip st to first dc: 40 dc.

**Rnd 7:** Ch 3, dc in next dc and in each dc around; join with slip st to first dc changing to Black, drop Red.

**Rnd 8:** With Black, ch 3, dc in next dc and in each dc around; join with slip st to first dc changing to Red, cut Black.

**Rnd 9:** Ch 3, dc in next dc and in each dc around; join with slip st to first dc.

**Rnd 10:** Ch 3, dc in next dc, dc2tog, (dc in next 2 dc, dc2tog) around; join with slip st to first dc: 30 dc.

**Rnd 11:** Ch 3, dc2tog, (dc in next dc, dc2tog) around; join with slip st to first dc: 20 dc.

Stuff Body very lightly with polyester fiberfill.

**Rnd 12:** Ch 2, dc in next dc, dc2tog around; skip beginning ch-2 and join with slip st to first dc changing to Cream, cut Red: 10 dc.

## HEAD

**Rnd 1:** Ch 3, dc in same st as joining, 2 dc in next dc and in each dc around; join with slip st to first dc: 20 dc.

**Rnds 2 and 3:** Ch 3, dc in next dc and in each dc around; join with slip st to first dc.

Stuff Head very lightly with polyester fiberfill.

**Rnd 4:** Ch 2, dc in next dc, dc2tog around; skip beginning ch-2 and join with slip st to first dc changing to White, cut Cream: 10 dc.

## HAT

**Rnd 1:** Work Beginning Popcorn in same st as joining, work Popcorn in next dc and in each dc around; join with slip st to top of Beginning Popcorn changing to Red, cut White: 10 Popcorns.

**Rnd 2:** Ch 3, 2 dc in next Popcorn, (dc in next Popcorn, 2 dc in next Popcorn) around; join with slip st to first dc: 15 dc.

**Rnd 3:** Ch 3, dc in next dc and in each dc around; join with slip st to first dc.

**Rnd 4:** Ch 3, dc2tog, (dc in next dc, dc2tog) around; join with slip st to first dc: 10 dc.

**Rnds 5 and 6:** Ch 3, dc in next dc and in each dc around; join with slip st to first dc; at end of Rnd 6, finish off.

**Rnd 7:** With **right** side facing, join White with slip st in same st as joining; work Beginning Popcorn in same st, skip next dc, (work Popcorn in next dc, skip next dc) around; join with slip st to top of Beginning Popcorn: 5 Popcorns.

**Rnd 8:** (Slip st, work Beginning Popcorn) in sp **before** next Popcorn ***(Fig. 5, page 31)***, (skip sp **before** next Popcorn, work Popcorn in sp **before** next Popcorn) twice; join with slip st to first dc, finish off.

## ARM (Make 2)

**Rnd 1** (Right side)**:** With Red, ch 4, 5 dc in fourth ch from hook **(3 skipped chs count as first dc)**; join with slip st to first dc: 6 dc.

***Note:*** Mark Rnd 1 as **right** side.

**Rnd 2:** Ch 3, dc in same st as joining, 2 dc in next dc and in each dc around; join with slip st to first dc: 12 dc.

**Rnds 3-6:** Ch 3, dc in next dc and in each dc around; join with slip st to first dc; at end of Rnd 6, finish off.

**CUFF & HAND**

**Rnd 1:** With **right** side facing, join White with slip st in same st as joining; work Beginning Popcorn in same st, skip next dc, (work Popcorn in next dc, skip next dc) around; join with slip st to first top of Beginning Popcorn: 6 Popcorns.

**Rnd 2:** Ch 3, dc in next ch-1 closing and in each Popcorn and ch-1 closing around; join with slip st to first dc, finish off leaving a 6" (15 cm) end for sewing: 12 dc.

Thread tapestry needle with end and weave through sts on Rnd 2 *(Fig. 6, page 31)*. Pull tightly to close and secure end.

**Arm Tie:** With Red and leaving a 4" (10 cm) end, ch 10; finish off leaving a 4" (10 cm) end. Thread ch through Rnd 1 of Arm and around any 2 dc on Rnd 11 of Body; tie ends together. Hide ends through Body.

For second Arm, skip 8 dc on Rnd 11 of Body and tie second Arm around next 2 dc in same manner.

## LEG (Make 2)

**Rnd 1** (Right side)**:** With Red, ch 4, 7 dc in fourth ch from hook **(3 skipped chs count as first dc)**; join with slip st to first dc: 8 dc.

*Note:* Mark Rnd 1 as **right** side.

**Rnd 2:** Ch 3, dc in same st as joining, 2 dc in next dc and in each dc around; join with slip st to first dc: 16 dc.

**Rnds 3-7:** Ch 3, dc in next dc and in each dc around; join with slip st to first dc; at end of Rnd 7, finish off.

### CUFF & FOOT

**Rnd 1:** With **right** side facing, join White with slip st in same st as joining; work Beginning Popcorn in same st, skip next dc, (work Popcorn in next dc, skip next dc) around; join with slip st to top of Beginning Popcorn, finish off: 8 Popcorns.

**Rnd 2:** With **right** side facing, skip Beginning Popcorn and join Black with slip st in sp **before** next Popcorn; ch 3, 3 dc in same sp, (skip next Popcorn, 4 dc in sp **before** next Popcorn) around; join with slip st to first dc: 32 dc.

**Rnd 3:** Ch 1, sc in same st as joining, skip next dc, (sc in next dc, skip next dc) around; join with slip st to first sc: 16 sc.

**Rnds 4 and 5:** Ch 1, sc in same st as joining, skip next sc, (sc in next sc, skip next sc) around; join with slip st to first sc: 4 sc.

Finish off leaving a 6" (15 cm) end for sewing.

Thread tapestry needle with end and weave through sts on Rnd 5; pull tightly to close and secure end.

**Leg Tie:** With Red and leaving a 4" (10 cm) end, ch 10; finish off leaving a 4" (10 cm) end. Thread ch through Rnd 1 of Leg and around 2 dc on Rnd 3 of Body that line up with Arm above; tie ends together. Hide ends through Body.

For second Leg, skip 13 dc on Rnd 3 of Body and tie second Leg around next 2 dc in same manner.

## BEARD

**Row 1** (Right side)**:** With White, ch 4, work (Popcorn, dc) in fourth ch from hook **(3 skipped chs counts as first dc)**: 2 dc and one Popcorn.

*Note:* Mark Row 1 as **right** side.

***To work a Popcorn*** on a **wrong** side row, insert hook from **back** to **front** so Popcorn with show on **right** side.

**Row 2:** Ch 3, turn; work Popcorn in first dc, work Popcorn in next Popcorn, work (Popcorn, dc) in last dc: 2 dc and 3 Popcorns.

**Row 3:** Ch 3, turn; work Popcorn in first dc, work Popcorn in each Popcorn across, work (Popcorn, dc) in last dc: 2 dc and 5 Popcorns.

**Row 4:** Ch 3, turn; work Popcorn in first Popcorn, work Popcorn in sp **before** each of next 4 Popcorns, work Popcorn in last Popcorn, dc in last dc: 2 dc and 6 Popcorns.

**Row 5:** Ch 3, turn; work Popcorn in first Popcorn, ch 3, ★ (slip st, work Beginning Popcorn) in next Popcorn, skip next Popcorn, slip st in sp **before** next Popcorn; repeat from ★ once **more**, (slip st, work Beginning Popcorn) in last Popcorn, dc in last dc; finish off.

Sew or glue Beard to face.
Sew seed beads to Face for eyes.

## HAIR

**Row 1** (Right side)**:** With White, ch 13, work Popcorn in fourth ch from hook **(3 skipped chs counts as first dc)**, dc in next ch, (work Popcorn in next ch, dc in next ch) across: 6 dc and 5 Popcorns.

**Rows 2 and 3:** Ch 3, turn; (work Popcorn in next Popcorn, dc in next dc) across; at end of Row 3, finish off.

Sew or glue Hair to back of Head.

**Hanger:** With Red and leaving a 4" (10 cm) end, ch 35; finish off leaving a 4" (10 cm) end. Attach hanger around a stitch on Rnd 3 of Hat; tie in a knot. Hide ends through Hat.

Using photo as a guide, page 8:
- Fold Hat to front and tack in place.
- Paint a buckle on Rnd 8 of Body.

*Design by Patricia Pogue.*

# STOCKING

EASY

**Finished Height:** Approximately 3½" (9 cm)

## SHOPPING LIST

**Thread** (Lace Weight) LACE 0

- ☐ Ecru - 30 yards (27.5 meters)
- ☐ Brown - 12 yards (11 meters)
- ☐ Red - Small amount

**Crochet Hook**

- ☐ Steel, size 1 (2.75 mm)

**Additional Supplies**

- ☐ ¼" (6 mm) Ribbon - 8" (20.5 cm) length

***Gauge is not important for this design.***

Stocking is made holding 2 strands of thread together throughout.

## TOE

With 2 strands of Ecru held together, ch 6; join with slip st to form a ring.

**Rnd 1** (Right side)**:** Ch 3 **(counts as first dc, now and throughout)**, 9 dc in ring; join with slip st to first dc: 10 dc.

*Note:* Loop a short piece of thread around any stitch to mark Rnd 1 as **right** side.

**Rnd 2:** Ch 3, dc in same st as joining, 2 dc in next dc and in each dc around, cut one strand of Ecru; holding one strand of Brown and remaining strand of Ecru together, join with slip st to first dc: 20 dc.

**Rnds 3-5:** Ch 3, dc in next dc and in each dc around; join with slip st to first dc; at end of Rnd 5, finish off.

## HEEL

**Row 1:** With **right** side facing, join 2 strands of Ecru with sc in same st as joining ***(see Joining With Sc, page 30)***; hdc in next dc, dc in next 7 dc, hdc in next dc, sc in next dc, leave remaining 9 dc unworked: 11 sts.

**Row 2:** Ch 1, turn; skip first sc, sc in next hdc, hdc in next dc, dc in next 5 dc, hdc in next dc, sc in next hdc changing to 2 strands of Red ***(Fig. 4a, page 31)***; cut Ecru, leave remaining sc unworked: 9 sts.

**Row 3:** Ch 1, turn; skip first sc, sc in next hdc, hdc in next dc, dc in next 3 dc, hdc in next dc, sc in next hdc changing to 2 strands of Ecru; cut Red, leave remaining sc unworked: 7 sts.

**Row 4:** Ch 1, turn; 2 sc in first sc, hdc in next hdc, dc in next 3 dc, hdc in next hdc, 2 sc in last sc: 9 sts.

**Row 5:** Ch 1, turn; 2 sc in first sc, hdc in next sc, dc in next 5 sts, hdc in next sc, 2 sc in last sc; finish off: 11 sts.

## BODY

**Rnd 1:** With **right** side facing, holding one strand of Brown and one strand of Ecru together, join thread with slip st in center dc on Row 5 of Heel; ch 3, dc in next 4 sts, YO, insert hook in last sc, YO and pull up a loop (3 loops on hook), pull up a loop in same dc as last sc on Row 1 of Heel (4 loops on hook), YO and draw through 3 loops on hook, YO and draw through remaining 2 loops on hook, dc in next 9 dc, YO, insert hook in same dc as first sc on Row 1 of Heel, YO and pull up a loop (3 loops on hook), pull up a loop in first sc on Row 5 of Heel (4 loops on hook), YO and draw through 3 loops on hook, YO and draw through remaining 2 loops on hook, dc in last 4 sts; join with slip st to first dc: 20 sts.

**Rnds 2 and 3:** Ch 3, dc in next st and in each st around; join with slip st to first dc.

**Rnd 4:** Ch 3, dc in next dc and in each dc around; cut Brown, holding one strand of Ecru and remaining strand of Ecru together, join with slip st to first dc.

## CUFF

**Rnds 1-3:** Ch 3, dc in next dc and in each dc around; join with slip st to first dc; at end of Rnd 3, finish off.

**Hanger:** Weave ribbon under 2 dc at back of Sock and tie ends in a knot.

*Design by Lula Sarka.*

# SANTA ORNAMENT

EASY

**Finished Height:** Approximately 3" (7.5 cm)

## SHOPPING LIST

### Thread (Lace Weight) LACE 0

- ☐ Pink - 40 yards (36.5 meters)
- ☐ White - 40 yards (36.5 meters)
- ☐ Red - 20 yards (18.5 meters)

### Crochet Hook

- ☐ Steel, size 9 (1.4 mm)

### Additional Supplies

- ☐ Tapestry needle
- ☐ Dk Pink & Black floss
- ☐ Polyester fiberfill
- ☐ Metallic thread

***Gauge is not important for this design.***

## STITCH GUIDE

**TREBLE CROCHET** ***(abbreviated tr)***

YO twice, insert hook in st indicated, YO and pull up a loop (4 loops on hook), (YO and draw through 2 loops on hook) 3 times.

**SINGLE CROCHET 2 TOGETHER** ***(abbreviated sc2tog)***

Pull up a loop in each of next 2 sc, YO and draw through all 3 loops on hook **(counts as one sc)**.

**DOUBLE CROCHET 2 TOGETHER** ***(abbreviated dc2tog)***

(uses next 2 dc)

★ YO, insert hook in **next** dc, YO and pull up a loop, YO and draw through 2 loops on hook; repeat from ★ once **more**, YO and draw through all 3 loops on hook **(counts as one dc)**.

**DOUBLE CROCHET 3 TOGETHER** ***(abbreviated dc3tog)***

(uses next 3 dc)

★ YO, insert hook in **next** dc, YO and pull up a loop, YO and draw through 2 loops on hook; repeat from ★ 2 times **more**, YO and draw through all 4 loops on hook **(counts as one dc)**.

## HEAD

**Rnd 1** (Right side)**:** With Pink, ch 2, 8 sc in second ch from hook; do **not** join, place a marker to indicate beginning of rnd ***(see Markers, page 30)***.

*Note:* Loop a short piece of thread around any stitch to mark Rnd 1 as **right** side.

**Rnd 2:** 2 Sc in each sc around: 16 sc.

**Rnd 3:** (Sc in next sc, 2 sc in next sc) around: 24 sc.

**Rnd 4:** (Sc in next 2 sc, 2 sc in next sc) around: 32 sc.

**Rnd 5:** (Sc in next 3 sc, 2 sc in next sc) around: 40 sc.

**Rnd 6:** Sc in each sc around.

**Rnd 7:** (Sc in next 4 sc, 2 sc in next sc) around: 48 sc.

**Rnd 8:** Sc in each sc around.

**Rnd 9:** (Sc in next 5 sc, 2 sc in next sc) around: 56 sc.

**Rnd 10:** Sc in each sc around.

**Rnd 11:** (Sc in next 6 sc, 2 sc in next sc) around: 64 sc.

**Rnd 12:** Sc in each sc around.

**Rnd 13:** (Sc in next 7 sc, 2 sc in next sc) around: 72 sc.

**Rnds 14-19:** Sc in each sc around.

**Rnd 20:** (Sc in next 7 sc, sc2tog) around: 64 sc.

**Rnd 21:** Sc in each sc around.

**Rnd 22:** (Sc in next 6 sc, sc2tog) around: 56 sc.

**Rnd 23:** Sc in each sc around.

**Rnd 24:** (Sc in next 5 sc, sc2tog) around: 48 sc.

**Rnd 25:** Sc in each sc around.

**Rnd 26:** (Sc in next 4 sc, sc2tog) around: 40 sc.

**Rnd 27:** Sc in each sc around.

**Rnd 28:** (Sc in next 3 sc, sc2tog) around: 32 sc.

**Rnd 29:** (Sc in next 2 sc, sc2tog) around: 24 sc.

Stuff Head with polyester fiberfill.

**Rnd 30:** (Sc in next sc, sc2tog) around: 16 sc.

**Rnd 31:** Sc2tog around; slip st in next st,
finish off leaving a long end for sewing.

Thread tapestry needle with end and weave through sts on Rnd 31 ***(Fig. 6, page 31)***. Pull tightly to close and secure end.

## HAT

With White and leaving a long end for sewing, ch 54; being careful **not** to twist ch, join with slip st to form a ring.

**Rnd 1** (Right side)**:** Ch 1, sc in same ch as joining and in each ch around; join with slip st to first sc: 54 sc.

*Note:* Mark Rnd 1 as **right** side.

**Rnd 2:** Ch 1, turn; sc in first sc, tr in next sc, (sc in next sc, tr in next sc) around; join with slip st to first sc.

**Rnd 3:** Ch 4 **(counts as first tr)**, do **not** turn; sc in next tr, (tr in next sc, sc in next tr) around; join with slip st to first tr.

**Rnd 4:** Ch 1, **turn**; sc in each st around; join with slip st to first sc changing to Red ***(Fig. 4b, page 31)***, cut White.

**Rnd 5:** Ch 3 **(counts as first dc, now and throughout)**, do **not** turn; dc in next sc and in each sc around; join with slip st to first dc.

**Rnd 6:** Ch 3, dc in next 3 dc, dc2tog, (dc in next 4 dc, dc2tog) around; join with slip st to first dc: 45 dc.

**Rnd 7:** Ch 3, dc in next dc and in each dc around; join with slip st to first dc.

**Rnd 8:** Ch 3, dc in next 2 dc, dc2tog, (dc in next 3 dc, dc2tog) around; join with slip st to first dc: 36 dc.

**Rnd 9:** Ch 3, dc in next dc and in each dc around; join with slip st to first dc.

**Rnd 10:** Ch 3, dc in next dc, dc2tog, (dc in next 2 dc, dc2tog) around; join with slip st to first dc: 27 dc.

**Rnd 11:** Ch 3, dc in next dc and in each dc around; join with slip st to first dc.

**Rnd 12:** Ch 3, dc2tog, (dc in next dc, dc2tog) around; join with slip st to first dc: 18 dc.

**Rnd 13:** Ch 3, dc in next dc and in each dc around; join with slip st to first dc.

**Rnd 14:** Ch 2, dc2tog, dc3tog 5 times; join with slip st to first dc, finish off leaving a long end for sewing: 6 dc.

Thread tapestry needle with end and weave through sts on Rnd 14. Pull tightly to close and secure end.

**POM-POM**

**Rnd 1** (Right side)**:** With White, ch 2, 8 sc in second ch from hook; do **not** join, place a marker to indicate beginning of rnd.

*Note:* Mark Rnd 1 as **right** side.

**Rnd 2:** 2 Sc in each sc around: 16 sc.

**Rnds 3-6:** Sc in each sc around.

**Rnd 7:** Sc2tog around: 8 sc.

Stuff Pom-pom lightly.

**Rnd 8:** Sc2tog around; finish off leaving a long end for sewing.

Thread tapestry needle with end and weave through sts on Rnd 8. Pull tightly to close and secure end; then sew to top of Hat.

Using photo as a guide for placement, page 12:

- With long end, sew Hat to top of Head.
- Add fringe to face for beard ***(Fig. E)***.
- Embroider Black eyes and Dk Pink nose.
- Add metallic thread hanger.

*Design by Joan Beebe.*

# FRINGE

Cut a piece of cardboard 3" (7.5 cm) square. Wind White thread around the cardboard until the card is filled, then cut across **both** ends, leaving 3" (7.5 cm) lengths.
Fold one strand in half. Using a steel crochet hook, draw the folded end around the desired stitch and pull the loose ends through the folded end ***(Fig. A)***; draw the knot up tightly. Repeat, referring to photo for placement. Trim ends as desired.

**Fig. A**

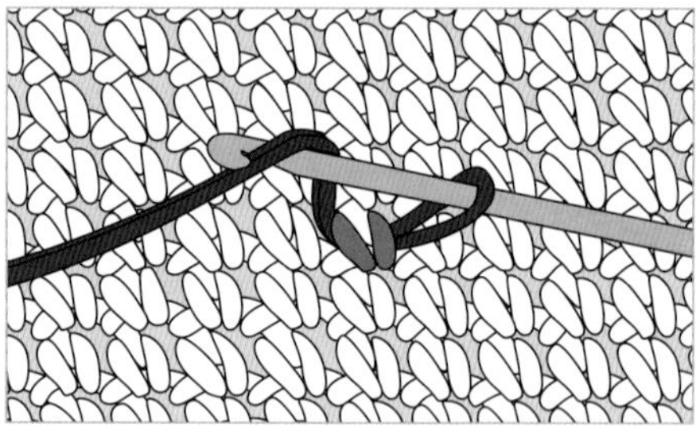

# DOLL PINS

EASY +

**Finished Height:** Approximately 4¼" (11 cm) (including Doll Pin & base)

## SHOPPING LIST

### Thread (Lace Weight) 0

**Santa**

- ☐ Red - 60 yards (55 meters)
- ☐ Black - 13 yards (12 meters)
- ☐ White - 8 yards (7.5 meters)

**Toy Soldier**

- ☐ Black - 25 yards (23 meters)
- ☐ Blue - 15 yards (13.5 meters)
- ☐ White - small amount
- ☐ Metallic Gold - small amount

### Crochet Hook

- ☐ Steel, size 6 (1.8 mm)

### Additional Supplies

- ☐ Doll pin - one for **each** design
- ☐ Craft glue
- ☐ Tapestry needle

## GAUGE INFORMATION

20 sc = 2" (5 cm)

## STITCH GUIDE

**SINGLE CROCHET 2 TOGETHER** *(abbreviated sc2tog)*

Pull up a loop in each of next 2 sc, YO and draw through all 3 loops on hook **(counts as one sc)**.

## SANTA

### PANTS

With Red, ch 16; being careful **not** to twist ch, join with slip st to form a ring.

**Rnd 1** (Right side)**:** Ch 1, sc in same ch as joining and in each ch around; join with slip st to first sc: 16 sc.

*Note:* Loop a short piece of thread around any stitch to mark Rnd 1 as **right** side.

**Rnd 2:** Ch 1, 2 sc in same st as joining and in each sc around; join with slip st to first sc: 32 sc.

### FIRST LEG

**Rnd 1:** Ch 5, skip next 15 sc, slip st in next sc, ch 1, sc in next 15 sc, skip next joining, sc in next 5 chs, skip next slip st; join with slip st to first sc: 20 sc.

**Rnds 2-12:** Ch 1, sc in same st as joining and in each sc around; join with slip st to first sc.

**Rnd 13:** Ch 1, sc in same st as joining and in next sc, sc2tog, (sc in next 2 sc, sc2tog) around; join with slip st to first sc, finish off: 15 sc.

**Rnd 14:** With **right** side facing and working in BLO ***(Fig. 2, page 30)***, join White with sc in same st as joining ***(see Joining With Sc, page 30)***; sc in each sc around; join with slip st to **both** loops of first sc.

**Rnd 15:** Ch 1, sc in both loops of same st as joining and in each sc around; join with slip st to first sc, finish off.

**Rnd 16:** With **right** side facing and working in BLO, join Black with sc in same st as joining; sc in each sc around; join with slip st to **both** loops of first sc.

**Rnds 17-22:** Ch 1, sc in both loops of same st as joining and in each sc around; join with slip st to first sc.

Finish off.

**SECOND LEG**

**Rnd 1:** With **right** side facing, join Red with sc in sc **before** joining (before ch-5); skip joining and sc in free loop of each ch across ***(Fig. 3b, page 30)***, skip next slip st and sc in each sc around; join with slip st to first sc: 20 sc.

Complete same as First Leg.

Put Pants carefully onto Doll Pin.

**COAT**

**Rnd 1** (Right side)**:** With Red, ch 12; being careful **not** to twist ch, join with slip st to form a ring.

*Note:* Mark Rnd 1 as **right** side.

**Rnd 2:** Ch 1, 2 sc in same st as joining and in each sc around; join with slip st to first sc: 24 sc.

**Rnd 3:** Ch 1, sc in same st as joining and in next 3 sc, ch 4, skip next 4 sc (armhole), sc in next 9 sc, ch 4, skip next 4 sc (armhole), sc in last 3 sc; join with slip st to first sc: 16 sc and 8 chs.

**Rnd 4:** Ch 1, sc in same st as joining and in next 3 sc, 2 sc in next ch, sc in next 2 chs, 2 sc in next ch, sc in next 9 sc, 2 sc in next ch, sc in next 2 chs, 2 sc in next ch, sc in last 3 sc; join with slip st to first sc: 28 sc.

**Rnds 5-8:** Ch 1, sc in same st as joining and in each sc around; join with slip st to first sc, at end of Rnd 8, finish off.

**Rnd 9:** With **right** side facing and working in BLO, join Black with sc in same st as joining; sc in each sc around; join with slip st to **both** loops of first sc.

**Rnd 10:** Ch 1, sc in both loops of same st as joining and in each sc around; join with slip st to first sc, finish off.

Begin working in rows.

**Row 1:** With **right** side facing, skip next 16 sc from joining and join Red with sc in next sc; sc in next 26 sc, leave last sc unworked: 27 sc.

**Rows 2-7:** Ch 1, turn; sc in each sc across; at end of Row 7, finish off.

**Trim:** With **right** side facing, join White with sc in last sc on Row 7; 2 sc in same st, sc in end of each row across and in unworked sc on Rnd 10, sc in end of each row across, 3 sc in first sc on Row 7, sc in each sc across; join with slip st to first sc, finish off.

**SLEEVE**

**Rnd 1:** With **right** side facing and working in free loops of chs at underarm, join Red with sc in first ch; sc in next 3 chs, (2 hdc, dc) in side of next sc, dc in each of 4 skipped sc, (dc, 2 hdc) in side of next sc; join with slip st to first sc: 14 sts.

**Rnds 2-9:** Ch 1, sc in same st as joining and in next 3 sc, hdc in next 2 hdc, dc in next 6 dc, hdc in next 2 hdc; join with slip st to first sc; at end of Rnd 9, finish off.

**Rnd 10:** With **right** side facing, join White with sc in same st as joining; sc in each st around; join with slip st to first sc, finish off.

**Rnd 11:** With **right** side facing and working in BLO, join Black with sc in same st as joining; sc in next 2 sc, sc2tog, sc in next 4 sc, sc2tog, sc in last 3 sc; join with slip st to **both** loops of first sc: 12 sc.

**Rnd 12:** Ch 1, working in both loops, sc in same st as joining, sc2tog, (sc in next sc, sc2tog) around; join with slip st to first sc: 8 sc.

**Rnd 13:** Ch 1, beginning in same st as joining, sc2tog around; join with slip st to first sc, finish off leaving a 6" (15 cm) end for sewing: 4 sc.

Thread tapestry needle with end and weave through sts on Rnd 13 ***(Fig. 6, page 31)***. Pull tightly to close and secure end.

Repeat for second Sleeve.

**COLLAR**

**Row 1:** With **right** side facing, join White with sc in sixth ch from joining; sc in each ch around; do **not** join: 12 sc.

**Rows 2:** Ch 1, turn; sc in each sc across; finish off.

Slip Coat over Doll Pin head. Glue in place at back of pin.

**HAT**

**Rnd 1** (Right side)**:** With Red, ch 2, 6 sc in second ch from hook; join with slip st to first sc.

*Note:* Mark Rnd 1 as **right** side.

**Rnds 2-4:** Ch 1, sc in same st as joining and in each sc around; join with slip st to first sc.

**Rnd 5:** Ch 1, sc in same st as joining and in next sc, 2 sc in next sc, sc in next 2 sc, 2 sc in next sc; join with slip st to first sc: 8 sc.

**Rnd 6:** Ch 1, sc in same st as joining and in each sc around; join with slip st to first sc.

**Rnd 7:** Ch 1, sc in same st as joining, 2 sc in next sc, (sc in next sc, 2 sc in next sc) around; join with slip st to first sc: 12 sc.

**Rnds 8-10:** Ch 1, sc in same st as joining and in each sc around; join with slip st to first sc.

**Rnd 11:** Ch 1, sc in same st as joining and in next sc, 2 sc in next sc, (sc in next 2 sc, 2 sc in next sc) around; join with slip st to first sc: 16 sc.

**Rnds 12-22:** Ch 1, sc in same st as joining and in each sc around; join with slip st to first sc, at end of Rnd 22, finish off.

**TRIM & BEARD**

**Rnd 1:** With **right** side facing, join White with sc in same st as joining; sc in each sc around; join with slip st to first sc: 16 sc.

**Rnd 2:** Ch 1, sc in same st as joining and in each sc around; join with slip st to first sc, ch 10, skip next 6 sc, slip st in next sc, finish off.

Cut 12 strands of White, each 2" (5 cm) long. Fold one strand in half. With **wrong** side facing and working in chs on Rnd 2, draw the folded end up through a ch and pull the loose ends through the folded end ***(Fig. A)***; draw the know up **tightly *(Fig. B)***. Repeat in each ch across for Beard. With remaining 2 strands held together, add to Rnd 1 of Hat for pom-pom.
Unravel each strand and trim as desired. Glue Hat to head of pin.

**Fig. A**

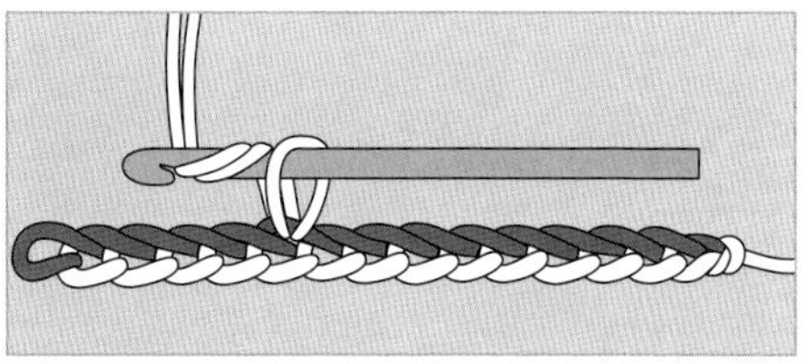

**Fig. B**

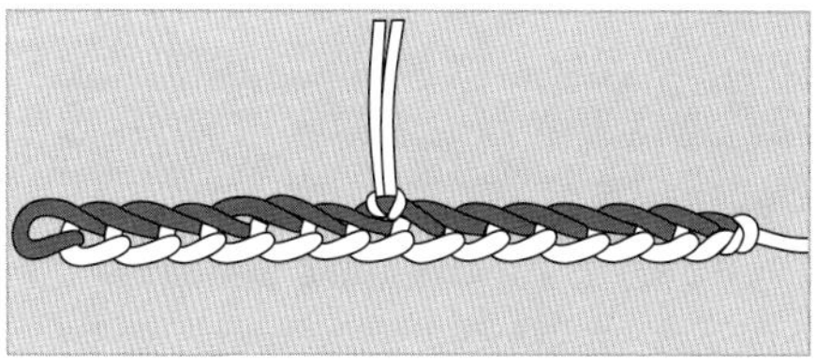

## TOY SOLDIER

### PANTS

With Black, ch 21; being careful **not** to twist ch, join with slip st to form a ring.

**Rnd 1** (Right side)**:** Ch 1, sc in same ch as joining and in each ch around; join with slip st to first sc: 21 sc.

*Note:* Mark Rnd 1 as **right** side.

### FIRST LEG

**Rnd 1:** Ch 5, skip next 10 sc, slip st in next sc, ch 1, sc in same ch and in next 9 chs, skip joining and sc in each ch across; join with slip st to first sc: 15 sc.

**Rnds 2-16:** Ch 1, sc in same st as joining and in each sc around; join with slip st to first sc, at end of Rnd 16, finish off.

### SECOND LEG

**Rnd 1:** With **right** side facing, join Black with sc in sc **before** joining (before ch-5); skip joining and sc in free loop of each ch across ***(Fig. 3b, page 30)***, skip next slip st and sc in each sc around; join with slip st to first sc: 15 sc.

Complete same as First Leg.

Put Pants carefully onto Doll Pin.

### SHIRT

With Blue, ch 16; being careful **not** to twist ch, join with slip st to form a ring.

**Rnd 1** (Right side)**:** Ch 1, sc in same ch and in next 7 chs, ch 1, skip next ch, sc in next ch and in each ch around; join with slip st to first sc: 15 sc and one ch-1 sp.

*Note:* Mark Rnd 1 as **right** side.

**Rnd 2:** Ch 1, sc in same st as joining, 2 sc in next sc, sc in next sc, ch 3, skip next 3 sc (armhole), sc in next sc, 2 sc in next sc, ch 1, skip next ch, sc in next sc, 2 sc in next sc, ch 3, skip next 3 sc (armhole), sc in next sc, 2 sc in last sc; join with slip st to first sc: 13 sc and 3 sps.

**Rnd 3:** Ch 1, **turn**; sc in same st as joining and in next 3 sc, sc in next 3 chs and in next 3 sc, ch 1, skip next ch, sc in next 3 sc and in next 3 chs, sc in last 3 sc; join with slip st to first sc: 19 sc and one ch-1 sp.

**Rnds 4-10:** Ch 1, turn; sc in same st as joining and in next 9 sc, ch 1, skip next ch, sc in last 9 sc; join with slip st to first sc, at end of Rnd 10, finish off leaving a long end for sewing.

### ARM

#### Shoulder Bar

**Rnd 1:** With Metallic Gold, ch 3; with **right** side of Shirt facing and neck opening toward you, slip st in center skipped sc of armhole and in next sc, ch 1, turn; working in ch-3 just made, sc in next 2 chs, 3 sc in last ch; working in free loops on opposite side of ch, sc in next 2 chs, slip st in next skipped sc of armhole and in end of Rnd 2 on Shirt: 7 sc.

**Rnd 2** (Right side)**:** Ch 1, turn; skip first 2 slip sts, sc in BLO of each sc on Shoulder Bar; slip st in end of Rnd 2 on Shirt, finish off.

**Sleeve**

**Rnd 1:** With **right** side of Shirt facing, working in free loops of chs at underarm, join Blue with sc in first ch; sc in next 2 chs, sc in next 7 sc on Shoulder Bar; do **not** join, place a marker to indicated beginning of rnd ***(see Markers, page 30)***: 10 sc.

**Rnds 2-10:** Sc in each sc around; at end of Rnd 10, slip st in next sc, finish off.

**Hand**

**Rnd 1:** With **right** side facing and working in BLO, join White with sc in any sc on Rnd 10 of Sleeve; sc in each sc around; join with slip st to **both** loops of first sc.

**Rnd 2:** Ch 1, sc in same st as joining and in each sc around; join with slip st to first sc.

**Rnd 3:** Ch 1, beginning in same st as joining, sc2tog around; join with slip st to first sc: 5 sc.

**Rnd 4:** Ch 1, beginning in same st as joining, sc2tog, sc in next sc, sc2tog; join with slip st to first sc, finish off leaving a 6" (15 cm) end for sewing.

Thread tapestry needle with end and weave through sts on Rnd 4. Pull tightly to close and secure end.

Repeat for second Arm.

**TRIM**

With **right** side facing, join Black with slip st around ch-1 on Rnd 10 of Shirt; working vertically on Shirt, slip st in each ch-1 sp across to neck; working in free loops of beginning ch, sc in each ch around neck; slip st in each ch-1 sp vertically back to Rnd 10; finish off.

Slip Shirt over Doll Pin head. With long end and having Trim at center front, sew Shirt to top of Pants.

**HAT**

**Rnd 1** (Right side)**:** With Black, ch 2, 8 sc in second ch from hook; join with slip st to first sc.

*Note:* Mark Rnd 1 as **right** side.

**Rnd 2:** Ch 1, 2 sc in same st as joining and in each sc around; join with slip st to BLO of first sc: 16 sc.

**Rnd 3:** Ch 1, sc in BLO of same st as joining and each sc around; join with slip st to **both** loops of first sc.

**Rnds 4-8:** Ch 1, sc in same st as joining and in each sc around; join with slip st to first sc.

**Strap & Brim:** Ch 11, skip next 10 sc on Rnd 8, slip st in next sc, turn; working in FLO of skipped sc, slip st in next 2 sc, sc in next sc, hdc in next 4 sc, sc in next sc, slip st in next 2 sc; finish off.

**Trim:** With **right** side facing and top of Hat toward you, join Metallic Gold with slip st in first free loop on Rnd 8; slip st in next 9 free loops; finish off.

Glue Hat to head of pin.

*Designs by Tammy Kreimeyer.*

# DOOR KNOB WREATH EASY

## SHOPPING LIST

### Thread (Lace Weight) LACE 0

- ☐ Red - 20 yards (18.5 meters)
- ☐ White - 10 yards (9 meters)

### Crochet Hook

- ☐ Steel, size 7 (1.65 mm)

### Additional Supplies

- ☐ $^7/_8$" (22 mm) Ribbon - 20"(51 cm) length

***Gauge is not important for this design.***

## STITCH GUIDE

**2-DC CLUSTER** (uses one sp)
★ YO, insert hook in sp indicated, YO and pull up a loop, YO and draw through 2 loops on hook; repeat from ★ once **more**, YO and draw through all 3 loops on hook.

**3-DC CLUSTER** (uses one sp)
★ YO, insert hook in sp indicated, YO and pull up a loop, YO and draw through 2 loops on hook; repeat from ★ 2 times **more**, YO and draw through all 4 loops on hook.

**PICOT**
Ch 5, slip st in fifth ch from hook.

## WREATH

With Red, ch 31.

**Row 1** (Right side)**:** 2 Hdc in third ch from hook and in each ch across; finish off: 58 hdc.

***Note:*** Loop a short piece of thread around any stitch to mark Row 1 as **right** side.

**Row 2:** With **right** side facing, join White with sc in first hdc ***(see Joining With Sc, page 30)***; ★ ch 5, skip next 2 hdc, sc in next hdc; repeat from ★ across: 19 ch-5 sps.

**Row 3:** Ch 7, turn; sc in first ch-5 sp, (ch 7, sc in next ch-5 sp) across.

**Row 4:** Ch 9, turn; sc in first ch-7 sp, (ch 9, sc in next ch-7 sp) across; finish off.

**Trim:** With **right** side facing, join Red with slip st in first ch-9 sp; ch 2, work 2-dc Cluster in same sp, work (Picot, 3-dc Cluster in same sp) twice, ★ work 3-dc Cluster in next ch-9 sp, work (Picot, 3-dc Cluster in same sp) twice; repeat from ★ across; finish off.

Thread ribbon through ch-7 sps at each end of Row 3; tie in a bow.

*Design by Alice E. Heim.*

# SANTA ORNAMENT & PIN

EASY

**Approximate Finished Height**
**Ornament:** 3¾" (9.5 cm)
**Pin:** 2¾" (7 cm)

## SHOPPING LIST

**Thread** (Lace Weight) LACE 0

**Ornament**

☐ Red - 35 yards (32 meters)
☐ White - 17 yards (15.5 meters)
☐ Peach - small amount
☐ Green - small amount

**Pin**

☐ Red - 17 yards (15.5 meters)
☐ White - 9 yards (8 meters)
☐ Peach - small amount
☐ Green - small amount

### Crochet Hook

☐ Steel, size 7 (1.65 mm)

### Additional Supplies

☐ Polyester fiberfill
☐ Tapestry needle
☐ Hot glue gun **or** craft glue

**Ornament**

☐ 4 mm round Black half beads (for eyes) - 2
☐ 3/8" (10 mm) Pom-pom
☐ Metallic thread (for hanger)

**Pin**

☐ 2 mm round Black half beads (for eyes) - 2
☐ ¼" (6 mm) Pom-pom
☐ 1" (25 mm) Pin back

## GAUGE INFORMATION

18 dc = 2" (5 cm)

## STITCH GUIDE

**HALF DOUBLE CROCHET 2 TOGETHER** ***(abbreviated hdc2tog)*** (uses next 2 sts)
★ YO, insert hook in **next** st, YO and pull up a loop; repeat from ★ once **more**, YO and draw through all 5 loops on hook **(counts as one hdc).**

**DOUBLE CROCHET 2 TOGETHER** ***(abbreviated dc2tog)*** (uses next 2 dc)
★ YO, insert hook in **next** dc, YO and pull up a loop, YO and draw through 2 loops on hook; repeat from ★ once **more**, YO and draw through all 3 loops on hook **(counts as one dc).**

## ORNAMENT

**BACK HEAD**

**Rnd 1** (Right side)**:** With White, ch 4, 11 dc in fourth ch from hook **(3 skipped chs count as first dc)**; join with slip st to first dc: 12 dc.

*Note:* Loop a short piece of thread around any stitch to mark Rnd 1 as **right** side.

**Rnd 2:** Ch 3 **(counts as first dc, now and throughout)**, dc in same st as joining, 2 dc in next dc and in each dc around; join with slip st to first dc: 24 dc.

**Rnd 3:** Ch 3, 2 dc in next dc, (dc in next dc, 2 dc in next dc) around; join with slip st to first dc, finish off: 36 dc.

**BACK BODY**

**Row 1:** With **right** side facing, join Red with slip st in next dc; ch 3, dc in same st, (hdc, sc) in next dc, 2 sc in each of next 2 dc, sc in next 2 dc, 2 sc in each of next 2 dc, (sc, hdc) in next dc, 2 dc in next dc, leave remaining 26 dc unworked: 18 sts.

**Rows 2 and 3:** Ch 3, **turn**; dc in first dc and in each st across to last dc, 2 dc in last dc: 22 dc.

**Rows 4-6:** Ch 3, turn; dc in next dc and in each dc across.

**Rows 7 and 8:** Ch 3, turn; dc2tog, dc in next dc and in each dc across to last 3 dc, dc2tog, dc in last dc: 18 dc.

**Row 9:** Ch 3, turn; dc2tog twice, dc in next 8 dc, dc2tog twice, dc in last dc; finish off: 14 dc.

**Edging:** With **right** side facing, join Red with slip st in end of Row 1; ch 1, 2 sc in end of same row and in each row across; sc in each dc across Row 9; 2 sc in end of each row across Back Body; finish off: 50 sc.

**FRONT HEAD**

**Rnd 1** (Right side)**:** With Peach, ch 4, 7 dc in fourth ch from hook **(3 skipped chs count as first dc)** changing to White in last dc made *(Fig. 4a, page 31)*, 4 dc in same ch; join with slip st to first dc: 12 dc.

**Rnd 2:** Ch 3, dc in same st as joining changing to Peach, 2 dc in each of next 6 dc changing to White in last dc made, 2 dc in each of last 5 dc; join with slip st to first dc: 24 dc.

Change colors in same manner throughout.

**Rnd 3:** Ch 3, 2 dc in BLO of next dc, with Peach, (dc in **both** loops of next dc, 2 dc in **both** loops of next dc) 6 times, cut Peach; with White, (dc in BLO of next dc, 2 dc in BLO of next dc) 5 times; join with slip st to first dc, finish off: 36 dc.

**FRONT BODY**

**Row 1:** With **right** side facing and working in BLO, join Red with slip st in 5th White dc after Peach; ch 3, dc in same st, (hdc, sc) in next dc, 2 sc in each of next 2 dc, sc in next 2 dc, 2 sc in each of next 2 dc, (sc, hdc) in next dc, 2 dc in next dc, leave remaining 26 dc unworked: 18 sts.

**Rows 2 and 3:** Ch 3, **turn**; working in both loops, dc in first dc and in each st across to last dc, 2 dc in last dc: 22 dc.

**Rows 4 and 5:** Ch 3, turn; dc in next dc and in each dc across.

**Row 6:** Ch 3, turn; dc in FLO of next dc and each dc across.

Working in **both** loops, complete same as Back Body.

**Joining Rnd:** With **wrong** sides together, Front facing and sts matching, and working through **inside** loops of **both** pieces, join Red with sc in first Red st *(see Joining With Sc, page 30)*; sc in each sc around Body changing to White in last sc made before Head, stuff Body lightly with polyester fiberfill; continuing to work through **inside** loops of **both** pieces, (sc, ch 3, hdc) in each White dc of Head, slip st in each st across to next White dc stuffing Head lightly with polyester fiberfill, (sc, ch 3, hdc) in each White dc; do **not** finish off.

**BEARD**

**Row 1:** Working in free loops of dc on Rnd 3 of Head *(Fig. 3a, page 30)*, sc in next dc, ch 3, hdc in top of last sc made, hdc in next dc, ch 3, hdc in top of last hdc made, (dc in next dc, ch 3, hdc in top of last dc made) 3 times, (dc, ch 3, hdc in top of last dc made) twice in next dc, (dc in next dc, ch 3, hdc in top of last dc made) 3 times, hdc in next dc, ch 3, hdc in top of last hdc made; join with slip st to first White sc on Edging, finish off.

**Row 2:** With **right** side facing, Head toward you and working in free loops of White sts on Rnd 2 of Head, join White with sc in first dc; ch 3, hdc in top of last sc made, sc in next dc, ch 3, hdc in top of last sc made, (dc in next dc, ch 3, hdc in top of last dc made) 4 times, (dc, ch 3, hdc in top of last dc made) twice in next dc, (dc in next dc, ch 3, hdc in top of last dc made) 3 times, hdc in next dc, ch 3, hdc in top of last hdc made, slip st in next dc; finish off.

**RIGHT ARM**

**Row 1:** With **right** side of Back facing and working in free loops of edging on Front Body, join Red with slip st in 9th sc before Head; ch 3, dc in next 6 sc: 7 sc.

**Row 2** (Right side)**:** Ch 3, turn; dc in next dc and in each dc across; finish off.

**Mitten**

**Row 1:** With **right** side facing, join Green with slip st in first dc; ch 3, dc in next dc and in each dc across: 7 dc.

**Row 2:** Ch 1, turn; sc in first dc, skip next 2 dc, 5 dc in next dc, skip next 2 dc, (sc, ch 2, sc) in last dc (thumb); finish off.

**LEFT ARM**

**Row 1:** With **right** side of Back facing and working in free loops of edging on Front Body, join Red with slip st in 3rd sc after Head; ch 3, dc in next 6 sc: 7 sc.

**Row 2** (Right side)**:** Ch 3, turn; dc in next dc and in each dc across; finish off.

**Mitten**

**Row 1:** With **right** side facing, join Green with slip st in first dc; ch 3, dc in next dc and in each dc across: 7 dc.

**Row 2:** Ch 1, turn; (sc, ch 2, sc) in first dc (thumb), skip next 2 dc, 5 dc in next dc, skip next 2 dc, sc in last dc; finish off.

**RUFFLE**

With **right** side of Front facing, Head toward you and working in free loops of Body Row 5, join White with slip st in first st; ch 3, hdc in same st, (slip st, ch 3, hdc) in each st across; finish off.

**HAT**

**Rnd 1** (Right side)**:** With Red, ch 4, 5 dc in fourth ch from hook **(3 skipped chs count as first dc)**; join with slip st to first dc: 6 dc.

*Note:* Mark Rnd 1 as **right** side.

**Rnd 2:** Ch 3, dc in same st as joining and in next dc, (2 dc in next dc, dc in next dc) twice; join with slip st to first dc: 9 dc.

**Rnd 3:** Ch 3, dc in next dc, 2 dc in next dc, (dc in next 2 dc, 2 dc in next dc) twice; join with slip st to first dc: 12 dc.

**Rnd 4:** Ch 3, dc in same st as joining and in next 3 dc, (2 dc in next dc, dc in next 3 dc) twice; join with slip st to first dc: 15 dc.

**Rnd 5:** Ch 3, dc in next 3 dc, 2 dc in next dc, (dc in next 4 dc, 2 dc in next dc) twice; join with slip st to first dc: 18 dc.

**Rnd 6:** Ch 3, dc in same st as joining and in next 5 dc, (2 dc in next dc, dc in next 5 dc) twice; join with slip st to first dc, finish off: 21 dc.

**Rnd 7:** With **right** side facing, join White with sc in same st as joining; sc in each dc around; join with slip st to first sc.

**Ruffle:** Ch 2, (slip st in next sc, ch 2) around; join with slip st to first slip st, finish off.

Using photo as a guide for placement, page 21:

- Glue pom-pom to tip of Hat, then sew or glue Hat to Head.
- Fold Hat to front and tack in place.
- Glue half beads to Head for eyes.
- Add metallic thread hanger.

## PIN

### BACK HEAD

**Rnds 1 and 2:** Work same as Ornament, page 21; at end of Rnd 2, finish off: 24 dc.

### BACK BODY

**Row 1:** With **right** side facing, join Red with slip st in next dc; ch 3, dc in same st, (hdc, sc) in next dc, sc in next 2 dc, (sc, hdc) in next dc, 2 dc in next dc, leave remaining 18 dc unworked: 10 sts.

**Rows 2 and 3:** Ch 3, **turn**; dc in first dc and in each st across to last dc, 2 dc in last dc: 14 dc.

**Row 4:** Ch 3, turn; dc in next dc and in each dc across.

**Rows 5 and 6:** Ch 3, turn; dc2tog, dc in next dc and in each dc across to last 3 dc, dc2tog, dc in last dc: 10 dc.

**Row 7:** Ch 2, turn; beginning in first dc, hdc2tog 5 times; finish off: 5 hdc.

**Edging:** With **right** side facing, join Red with slip st in end of Row 1; ch 1, 2 sc in end of same row and in each row across; sc in each hdc across Row 7; 2 sc in end of each row across Body; finish off: 33 sc.

### FRONT HEAD

Work same as Ornament, page 22; at end of Rnd 2, finish off: 24 dc.

### FRONT BODY

**Row 1:** With **right** side facing and working in BLO, join Red with slip in 4th White dc after Peach; ch 3, d in same st, (hdc, sc) in next dc, sc next 2 dc, (sc, hdc) in next dc, 2 d in next dc, leave remaining 18 dc unworked: 10 sts.

**Rows 2 and 3:** Ch 3, **turn**; dc in first dc and in each st across to last dc, 2 dc in last dc: 14 dc.

**Row 4:** Ch 3, turn; working in FLO, dc in next dc and each dc across.

Working in **both** loops, complete same as Back Body.

**Joining Rnd:** With **wrong** sides together, Front facing and sts matching, and working through **inside** loops of **both** pieces, join Red with sc in first Red st; sc in each sc around Body changing to White in last sc made before Head, stuff Body lightly with polyester fiberfill; continuing to work through **inside** loops of **both** pieces, (sc, ch 3, hdc) in each White dc of Head, slip st in each st across to next White dc stuffing Head lightly with polyester fiberfill, (sc, ch 3, hdc) 3 times; working in free loops on Rnd 2 of Head (to form Beard), (slip st, ch 2, sc) in first 2 dc, in next st work **[**sc, ch 2, hdc in top of last sc made, dc, ch 2, hdc in top of last dc made**]**, in next st work **[**dc, ch 3, hdc in top of last dc made, hdc, ch 2, hdc in top of last hdc made**]**, sc in next st, ch 2, sc in top of last sc made, sc in next st, ch 2, slip st in top of last sc made; join with slip st to first White sc, finish off.

### RIGHT ARM

**Row 1:** With **right** side of Back facing and working in free loops of edging on Front Body, join Red with slip st in 5th sc before Head; ch 3, dc in next 3 sc: 4 sc.

**Row 2** (Right side)**:** Ch 3, turn; dc in next dc and in each dc across; finish off.

**Right Mitt**

**Row 1:** With **wrong** side facing, join Green with slip st in first dc; 3 dc in next dc, skip next dc, slip st in last dc; finish off.

**LEFT ARM**

**Row 1:** With **right** side of Back facing and working in free loops of edging on Front Body, join Red with slip st in 2nd sc after Head; ch 3, dc in next 3 sc: 4 sc.

**Row 2** (Right side)**:** Ch 3, turn; dc in next dc and in each dc across; finish off.

**Left Mitt**

Work same as Right Mitt.

**RUFFLE**

With **right** side of Front facing, Head toward you and working in free loops of Body Row 3, join White with slip st in first st; ch 3, hdc in same st, (slip st, ch 3, hdc) in each st across; finish off.

**HAT**

**Rnd 1** (Right side)**:** With Red, ch 4, 5 dc in fourth ch from hook **(3 skipped chs count as first dc)**; join with slip st to first dc: 6 dc.

*Note:* Mark Rnd 1 as **right** side.

**Rnd 2:** Ch 3, dc in same st as joining and in next dc, (2 dc in next dc, dc in next dc) twice; join with slip st to first dc: 9 dc.

**Rnd 3:** Ch 3, dc in next dc, 2 dc in next dc, (dc in next 2 dc, 2 dc in next dc) twice; join with slip st to first dc: 12 dc.

**Rnd 4:** Ch 3, dc in same st as joining and in next 3 dc, (2 dc in next dc, dc in next 3 dc) twice; join with slip st to first dc, finish off: 15 dc.

**Ruffle:** With **right** side facing, join White with sc in same st as joining; ch 2, ★ (sc, ch 2) twice in next sc, sc in next st, ch 2; repeat from ★ around; join with slip st to first sc, finish off.

Using photo as a guide for placement:

- Glue pom-pom to tip of Hat, then sew or glue Hat to Head.
- Fold Hat to front and tack in place.
- Glue half beads to Head for eyes.
- Glue or sew pin back to back of Body.

*Designs by Dianne Bee.*

# SNOWMAN ORNAMENT & PIN

EASY

**Approximate Finished Height**

**Ornament:** 3¾" (9.5 cm) tall

**Pin:** 2¾" (7 cm) tall

## SHOPPING LIST

### Thread (Lace Weight) LACE 0

**Ornament**

- ☐ White - 35 yards (32 meters)
- ☐ Black - 5 yards (4.5 meters)

**Pin**

- ☐ White - 18 yards (16.5 meters)
- ☐ Black - small amount

### Crochet Hook

- ☐ Steel, size 7 (1.65 mm)

### Additional Supplies

- ☐ Polyester fiberfill
- ☐ Tapestry needle
- ☐ Hot glue gun **or** craft glue

**Ornament**

- ☐ 4 mm round Black half beads (for eyes) - 2
- ☐ 8 mm Black sequins (for buttons) - 3
- ☐ 5/8" (16 mm) Wire-edged ribbon - 8" (20.5 cm) length
- ☐ Metallic thread (for hanger)

**Pin**

- ☐ 2 mm round Black half beads (for eyes) - 2
- ☐ 4 mm round Black half beads (for buttons) - 3
- ☐ 3/8" (10 mm) Ribbon - 6" (15 cm) length
- ☐ 1" (25 mm) Pin back

## GAUGE INFORMATION

18 dc = 2" (5 cm)

## STITCH GUIDE

**DOUBLE CROCHET 2 TOGETHER** ***(abbreviated dc2tog)***

(uses next 2 dc)

★ YO, insert hook in **next** dc, YO and pull up a loop, YO and draw through 2 loops on hook; repeat from ★ once **more**, YO and draw through all 3 loops on hook **(counts as one dc)**.

## ORNAMENT

**HEAD & BODY** (Make 2)

**Rnd 1** (Right side)**:** With White, ch 4, 11 dc in fourth ch from hook **(3 skipped chs count as first dc)**; join with slip st to first dc: 12 dc.

*Note:* Loop a short piece of thread around any stitch on Rnd 1 to mark **right** side.

**Rnd 2:** Ch 3 **(counts as first dc, now and throughout)**, dc in same st as joining, 2 dc in next dc and in each dc around; join with slip st to first dc: 24 dc.

**Rnd 3:** Ch 3, 2 dc in next dc, (dc in next dc, 2 dc in next dc) around; join with slip st to first dc: 36 dc.

Begin working in rows.

**Row 1:** Ch 3, dc in same st as joining, (hdc, sc) in next dc, 2 sc in each of next 2 dc, sc in next 2 dc, 2 sc in each of next 2 dc, (sc, hdc) in next dc, 2 dc in next dc, leave remaining 26 dc unworked: 18 sts.

**Rows 2 and 3:** Ch 3, **turn**; dc in first dc and in each st across to last dc, 2 dc in last dc: 22 dc.

**Rows 4-6:** Ch 3, turn; dc in next dc and in each dc across.

**Rows 7 and 8:** Ch 3, turn; dc2tog, dc in next dc and in each dc across to last 3 dc, dc2tog, dc in last dc: 18 dc.

**Row 9:** Ch 3, turn; dc2tog twice, dc in next 8 dc, dc2tog twice, dc in last dc: 14 dc.

**Edging Rnd:** Ch 1, do **not** turn; 2 sc in end of each row across; sc in remaining 26 dc of Rnd 3; 2 sc in end of each row across; sc in each dc across Row 9; join with slip st to first sc: 76 sc.

Finish off on first piece; do **not** finish off at end of Edging Rnd on second piece.

**Joining Rnd:** Ch 1, with **wrong** sides together, sts matching and working through **inside** loops of **both** pieces, sc in each sc around, stuffing Head & Body lightly with polyester fiberfill before closing; join with slip st to first sc, finish off.

**HAT**

**Rnd 1** (Right side)**:** With Black, ch 6, 2 sc in second ch from hook, sc in next 3 chs, 3 sc in last ch; working in free loops of beginning ch ***(Fig. 3b, page 30)***, sc in next 4 chs; join with slip st to BLO of first sc ***(Fig. 2, page 30)***: 12 sc.

*Note:* Mark Rnd 1 as **right** side.

**Rnd 2:** Ch 3, working in BLO, dc in same st as joining and in next 5 sc, 2 dc in next sc, dc in last 5 sc; join with slip st to first dc: 14 dc.

**Rnd 3:** Ch 3, working in both loops, dc in same st as joining and in next 6 dc, 2 dc in next dc, dc in last 6 dc; join with slip st to first dc: 16 dc.

**Rnd 4:** Ch 3, dc in same st as joining, 2 dc in next dc and in each dc around; join with slip st to first dc, finish off leaving a long end for sewing.

Using photo as a guide for placement:

- Sew or glue Hat to Head.
- Glue sequins to Body for buttons and half beads to Head for eyes.
- Tie ribbon around neck; trim as desired.
- Add metallic thread hanger.

## PIN

**HEAD & BODY** (Make 2)

**Rnds 1 and 2:** Work same as Ornament, page 26: 24 dc.

Begin working in rows.

**Row 1:** Ch 3, hdc in same st as joining, (hdc, sc) in next dc, 2 sc in next dc, sc in next dc, 2 sc in next dc, (sc, hdc) in next dc, (hdc, dc) in next dc, leave remaining 17 dc unworked: 13 sts.

**Row 2:** Ch 3, **turn**; dc in same st as joining, dc in next 11 sts, 2 dc in last dc: 15 dc.

**Rows 3 and 4:** Ch 3, turn; dc in next dc and in each dc across.

**Rows 5 and 6:** Ch 3, turn; dc2tog, dc in next dc and in each dc across to last 3 sts, dc2tog, dc in last dc: 11 dc.

**Edging Rnd:** Ch 1, turn; sc in each dc across; 2 sc in end of each row across; sc in remaining 17 dc of Rnd 2; 2 sc in end of each row across; join with slip st to first sc: 52 sc.

Finish off on first piece; do **not** finish off at end of Edging Rnd on second piece.

**Joining Rnd:** Ch 1, with **wrong** sides together, sts matching and working through **inside** loops of **both** pieces, sc in each sc around, stuffing Head & Body lightly with polyester fiberfill before closing; join with slip st to first sc, finish off.

**HAT**

**Rnd 1** (Right side)**:** With Black, ch 6, 2 sc in second ch from hook, sc in next 3 chs, 3 sc in last ch; working in free loops of beginning ch ***(Fig. 3b, page 30)***, sc in next 4 chs; join with slip st to BLO of first sc ***(Fig. 2, page 30)***: 12 sc.

*Note:* Mark Rnd 1 as **right** side.

**Rnd 2:** Ch 3, dc in BLO of next sc and each sc around; join with slip st to first dc.

**Rnd 3:** Ch 3, dc in both loops of next dc and each dc around; join with slip st to first dc.

**Rnd 4:** Ch 3, dc in same st as joining, 2 dc in next dc and in each dc around; join with slip st to first dc, finish off leaving a long end for sewing.

Using photo as a guide for placement, page 27:

- Sew or glue Hat to Head.
- Glue 4 mm half beads to Body for buttons and 2 mm half beads to Head for eyes.
- Tie ribbon around neck; trim as desired.
- Glue or sew pin back to back of Body.

*Designs by Dianne Bee.*

# HOLLY LAPEL PIN

EASY

## SHOPPING LIST

**Thread** (Lace Weight) LACE 0

☐ Green - 6 yards (5.5 meters)

☐ Red - small amount

**Crochet Hook**

☐ Steel, size 9 (1.4 mm)

**Additional Supplies**

☐ Small safety pin

☐ Tapestry needle

***Gauge is not important for this design.***

## LEAF (Make 3)

**Row 1** (Right side)**:** With Green, ch 4, 6 dc in fourth ch from hook **(3 skipped chs count as first dc)**: 7 dc.

*Note:* Loop a short piece of thread around any stitch to mark Row 1 as **right** side.

**Row 2:** Ch 1, turn; sc in first dc, hdc in next dc, dc in next 3 dc, hdc in next dc, sc in last dc.

**Row 3:** Turn; slip st in first 4 sts, ch 3 **(counts as first dc)**, 6 dc in same st: 7 dc.

**Row 4:** Ch 1, turn; sc in first dc, hdc in next dc, dc in next 3 dc, hdc in next dc, sc in last dc.

**Row 5:** Turn; slip st in first 3 sts, ch 2, ★ YO, insert hook in **next** dc, YO and pull up a loop, YO and draw through 2 loops on hook; repeat from ★ once **more**, YO and draw through all 3 loops on hook; finish off.

## BERRY (Make 3)

**Rnd 1:** Ch 2, 8 sc in second ch from hook; do **not** join, place marker to indicated beginning of round *(**see Markers, page 30**)*.

**Rnd 2:** ★ Pull up a loop in each of next 2 sc, YO and draw through all 3 loops on hook; repeat from ★ around; finish off leaving a long end for sewing: 4 sts.

Thread tapestry needle with end and weave through sts on Rnd 2; pull tightly to close. Using same end, sew to Row 1 of Leaf.

Using photo as a guide for placement, sew Leaves together while sewing safety pin to **wrong** side.

*Design by Joan Beebe.*

# General Instructions

## ABBREVIATIONS

| | |
|---|---|
| BLO | Back Loop(s) Only |
| ch(s) | chain(s) |
| cm | centimeters |
| dc | double crochet(s) |
| dc2tog | double crochet 2 together |
| dc3tog | double crochet 3 together |
| FLO | Front Loop(s) Only |
| hdc | half double crochet(s) |
| hdc2tog | half double crochet 2 together |
| mm | millimeters |
| Rnd(s) | Round(s) |
| sc | single crochet(s) |
| sc2tog | single crochet 2 together |
| st(s) | stitch(es) |
| tr | treble crochet |
| YO | yarn over |

## SYMBOLS & TERMS

★ — work instructions following ★ as many **more** times as indicated in addition to the first time.

( ) or **[ ]** — work enclosed instructions **as many** times as specified by the number immediately following **or** work all enclosed instructions in the stitch or space indicated **or** contains explanatory remarks.

colon (:) — the number(s) given after a colon at the end of a row or round denote(s) the number of stitches or spaces you should have on that row or round.

## GAUGE

All of the instructions are written for bedspread weight cotton thread (size 10). Gauge is not important for most of the projects; your project may be a little larger or smaller without changing the overall effect. When a gauge is given in the individual instructions, make a sample swatch in the thread and hook specified. If your swatch is larger or smaller than specified, **make another, changing hook size to get the correct gauge.** Keep trying until you find the size hook that will give you the specified gauge.

| Yarn Weight Symbol & Names | LACE 0 | SUPER FINE 1 | FINE 2 | LIGHT 3 | MEDIUM 4 | BULKY 5 | SUPER BULKY 6 | JUMBO 7 |
|---|---|---|---|---|---|---|---|---|
| Type of Yarns in Category | Fingering, size 10 crochet thread | Sock, Fingering, Baby | Sport, Baby | DK, Light Worsted | Worsted, Afghan, Aran | Chunky, Craft, Rug | Super Bulky, Roving | Jumbo, Roving |
| Crochet Gauge* Ranges in Single Crochet to 4" (10 cm) | 32-42 sts** | 21-32 sts | 16-20 sts | 12-17 sts | 11-14 sts | 8-11 sts | 6-9 sts | 5 sts and fewer |
| Advised Hook Size Range | Steel*** 6 to 8, Regular hook B-1 | B-1 to E-4 | E-4 to 7 | 7 to I-9 | I-9 to K-10½ | K-10½ to M/N-13 | M/N-13 to Q | Q and larger |

*GUIDELINES ONLY: The chart above reflects the most commonly used gauges and hook sizes for specific yarn categories.

** Lace weight yarns are usually crocheted with larger hooks to create lacy openwork patterns. Accordingly, a gauge range is difficult to determine. Always follow the gauge stated in your pattern.

*** Steel crochet hooks are sized differently from regular hooks–the higher the number, the smaller the hook, which is the reverse of regular hook sizing.

| CROCHET TERMINOLOGY | | |
|---|---|---|
| UNITED STATES | | INTERNATIONAL |
| slip stitch (slip st) | = | single crochet (sc) |
| single crochet (sc) | = | double crochet (dc) |
| half double crochet (hdc) | = | half treble crochet (htr) |
| double crochet (dc) | = | treble crochet (tr) |
| treble crochet (tr) | = | double treble crochet (dtr) |
| double treble crochet (dtr) | = | triple treble crochet (ttr) |
| triple treble crochet (tr tr) | = | quadruple treble crochet (qtr) |
| skip | = | miss |

## MARKERS

Markers are used to help distinguish the beginning of each round being worked. Place a 2" (5 cm) scrap piece of thread before the first stitch of each round, moving marker after each round is complete.

## JOINING WITH SC

When instructed to join with a sc, begin with a slip knot on the hook. Insert hook in stitch or space indicated, YO and pull up a loop, YO and draw through both loops on hook.

## JOINING WITH DC

When instructed to join with a dc, begin with a slip knot on the hook. YO, holding loop on hook, insert hook in stitch or space indicated, YO and pull up a loop (3 loops on hook), (YO and draw through 2 loops on hook) twice.

## BACK RIDGE OF A CHAIN

Work only in loops indicated by arrows ***(Fig. 1)***.

**Fig. 1**

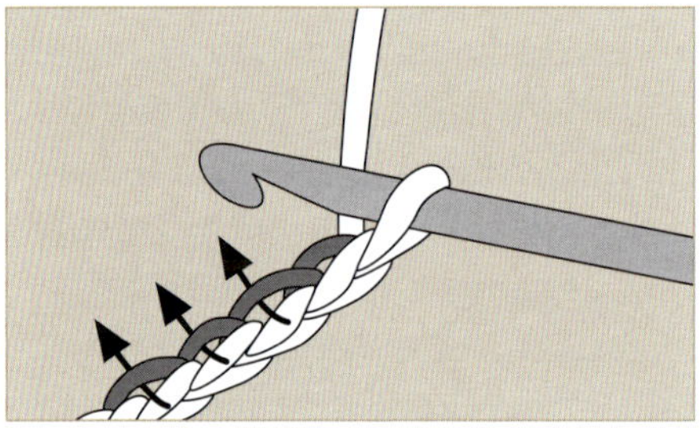

## BACK OR FRONT LOOP ONLY

Work only in loop(s) indicated by arrow ***(Fig. 2)***.

**Fig. 2**

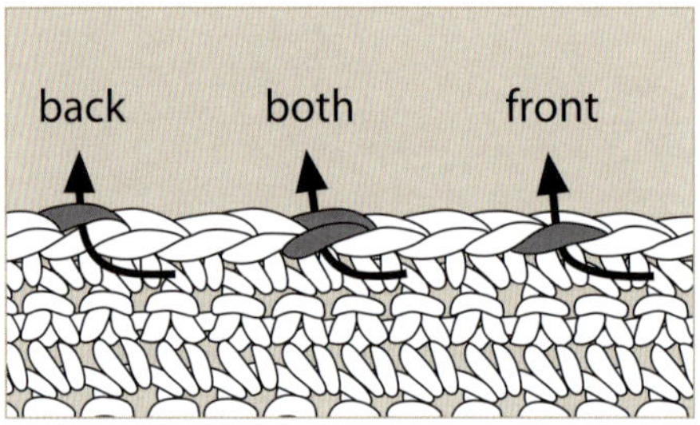


## FREE LOOPS

After working in Back or Front Loops Only on a row or round, there will be a ridge of unused loops. These are called the free loops. Later, when instructed to work in the free loops of the same row or round, work in these loops ***(Fig. 3a)***.

When instructed to work in free loops of a chain, work in loop indicated by arrow ***(Fig. 3b)***.

**Fig. 3a**

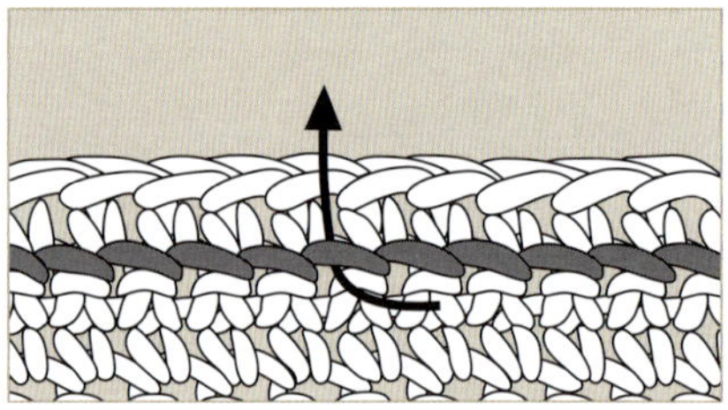

**Fig. 3b**

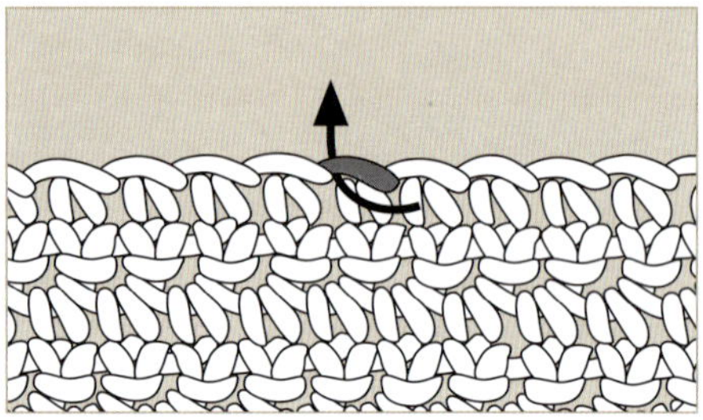

| STEEL CROCHET HOOKS | | | | | | | | | | | | | | | | |
|---|---|---|---|---|---|---|---|---|---|---|---|---|---|---|---|---|
| **U.S.** | 00 | 0 | 1 | 2 | 3 | 4 | 5 | 6 | 7 | 8 | 9 | 10 | 11 | 12 | 13 | 14 |
| **Metric - mm** | 3.5 | 3.25 | 2.75 | 2.25 | 2.1 | 2 | 1.9 | 1.8 | 1.65 | 1.5 | 1.4 | 1.3 | 1.1 | 1 | .85 | .75 |

|  |  |
|---|---|
| **BEGINNER** | Projects for first-time crocheters using basic stitches. Minimal shaping. |
| **EASY** | Projects using yarn with basic stitches, repetitive stitch patterns, simple color changes, and simple shaping and finishing. |
| **INTERMEDIATE** | Projects using a variety of techniques, such as basic lace patterns or color patterns, mid-level shaping and finishing. |
| **EXPERIENCED** | Projects with intricate stitch patterns, techniques and dimension, such as non-repeating patterns, multi-color techniques, fine threads, small hooks, detailed shaping and refined finishing. |

# CHANGING COLORS

Work the last stitch to within one step of completion, hook new yarn ***(Figs. 4a or 4b)*** and draw through all loops on hook.

**Fig. 4a**

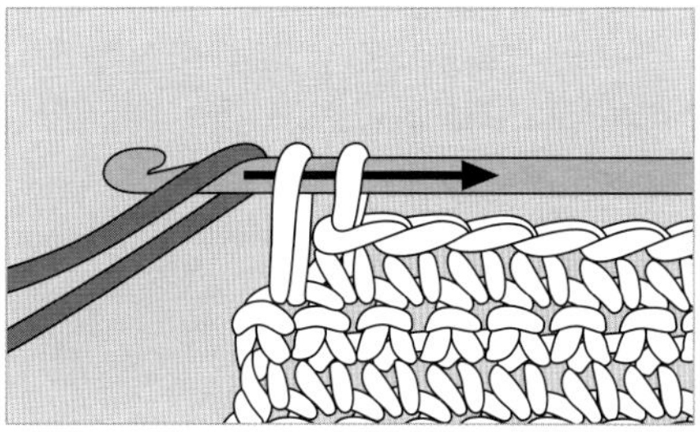

**Fig. 4b**

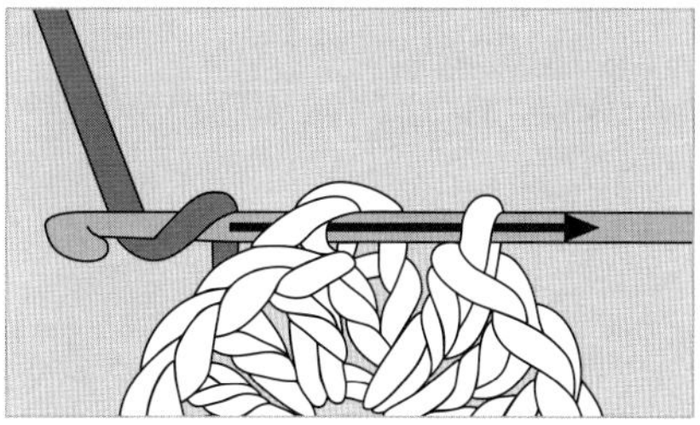

# WORKING IN A SPACE BEFORE A STITCH

When instructed to work in space before a stitch or in spaces between stitch, insert hook in space indicated by arrow ***(Fig. 5)***.

**Fig. 5**

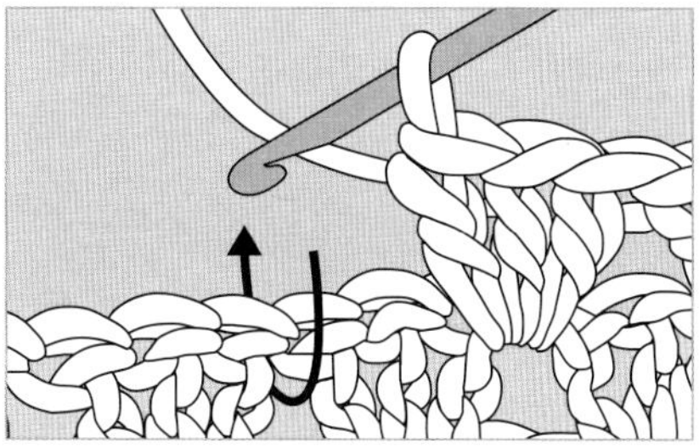

# WEAVE THRU STITCHES

Weave thread end through the stitches ***(Fig. 6)*** and gather to close.

**Fig. 6**

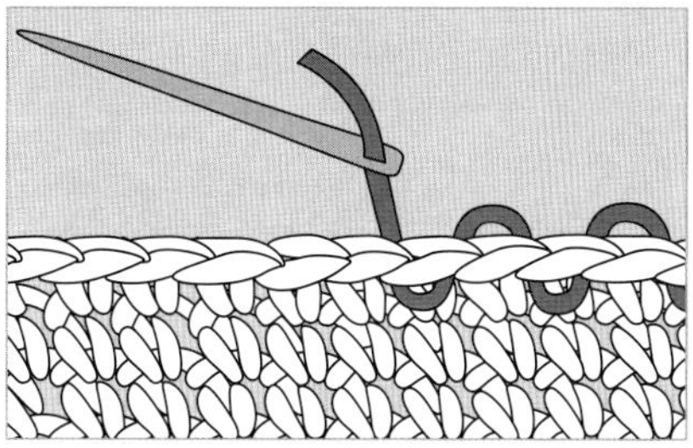

# EMBROIDERY STITCHES

## Straight Stitch

Straight stitch is just what the name implies, a single, straight stitch. Come up at 1 and go down at 2 ***(Fig. 7)***.

**Fig. 7**

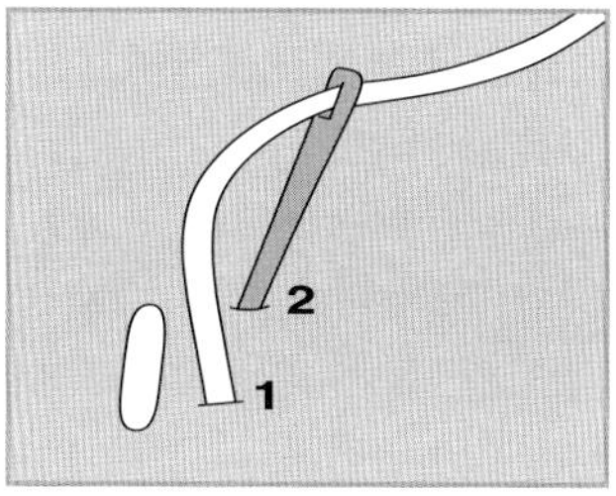


## French Knot

Bring needle up at 1. Wrap yarn around needle once and insert needle at 2, holding end of thread with non-stitching fingers ***(Fig. 8)***. Tighten knot; then pull needle through, holding thread until it must be released.

**Fig. 8**

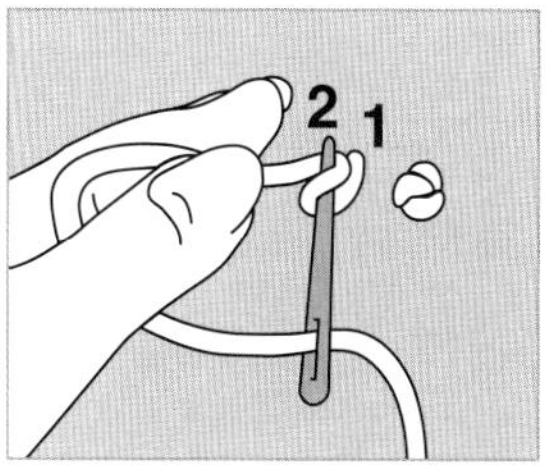

# Thread Information

The projects in this book were made using Lace Weight thread. Any brand of Bedspread Weight (size 10) thread may be used.

For your convenience, listed below are the specific threads and colors used to create our photography models. Because thread manufacturers make frequent changes in their product lines, you may sometimes find it necessary to use a substitute thread or to search for the discontinued product at alternate suppliers (locally or online).

### OOPS! DROPPED HER HALO ANGEL ORNAMENT

*Aunt Lydia's® Classic 10™*
White - #1 White
Metallic Gold - #90G Gold/Gold
Cream - #420 Cream

### REINDEER ORNAMENT

*Aunt Lydia's® Classic 10™*
Brown - #131 Fudge Brown
Black - #12 Black
Off White - #210 Antique White
Red - #494 Victory Red

### MINI CLOTHESPIN ANGEL

*DMC® Cebelia Size 10*
White - White
Red - #666
Green - #699

### DANGLE SANTA

*Aunt Lydia's® Classic 10™*
Red - #196 Cardinal
White - #1 White
Cream - #420 Cream
Black - #12 Black

### STOCKING

*Aunt Lydia's® Classic 10*
Ecru - #419 Ecru
Brown - #131 Fudge Brown
Red - #494 Victory Red

### SANTA ORNAMENT

*DMC® Cebelia Size 10*
Pink - #818
White - White
Red - #666

### DOLL PINS

*Aunt Lydia's® Classic 10™*
**Santa**
Red - #196 Cardinal
Black - #12 Black
White - #1 White
**Toy Soldier**
Black - #12 Black
Blue - #480 Delft
White - #1 White
Metallic Gold - #90G Gold/Gold

### DOOR KNOB WREATH

*DMC® Cebelia Size 10*
Red - #666
White - White

### SANTA ORNAMENT & PIN

*Aunt Lydia's® Classic 10™*
Red - #492 Burgundy
White - #1 White
Peach - #424 Light Peach
*DMC® Cebelia Size 10*
Green - #699

### SNOWMAN ORNAMENT & PIN

*Aunt Lydia's® Classic 10™*
White - #1 White
Black - #12 Black

### HOLLY LAPEL PIN

*DMC® Cebelia Size 10*
Green - #699
Red - #666

We have made every effort to ensure that these instructions are accurate and complete. We cannot, however, be responsible for human error, typographical mistakes, or variations in individual work.

Production Team: Instructional/Technical Editor - Linda A. Daley; Editorial Writer - Susan Frantz Wiles; Senior Graphic Artist - Lora Puls; Graphic Artist - Leia Morshedi; Photo Stylist - Marcus Boyce; and Photographer - Ken West.

Projects made and instructions tested by Barbara Schou.



Made In U.S.A.